Conte:

Credits

Game development, cartography, and character sheet by **Paul Baldowski**

Cover adapted from **Henry Gillard Glindoni**; Interior Illustrations by **Evlyn Moreau**

Lost in Translation by **Paul Baldowski**, adapted from an adventure by **Graham Ward**

Brainstorming, Feedback and Additional writing by **Richard August** and **Simon Taylor**

All due attribution and appreciative nod to *Maze Rats*, CC BY 4.0, and **Ben Milton**

Thanks to all the playtesters across eight years and many conventions

Copyright © 2021 **Paul Baldowski** | First print edition published **April 2021**

The Sanction of Magick

When **Elizabeth Tudor** succeeded to the throne in **1558**, she found herself under assault from all sides, challenged by the legacy of her family's actions.

Henry VIII severed ties with the **Church of Rome**. He made himself an enemy of Catholicism. Later, **Elizabeth**'s half-sister **Mary** sought to undo their father's work. Amid widespread religious reform, upheaval in the palaces and pastures of Europe, and the spread of the written word of **Protestant** belief, God grew distant.

The barrier created by a wall of blind faith, maintained over centuries by the Church's strength, wavered. The wider population saw the resurgence of **bugs** and the **Fae** as a byproduct of the malefic acts enacted by the opposing sides—**Catholics** and **Protestants**.

In **1563**, the Queen passed an **Act Against Conjurations, Enchantments and Witchcraft**. It made magick use to kill another a capital offence—triggered in no small part by a **Catholic** plot to assassinate the **Queen** through sorcery two years earlier. It also made a felony of the use of magick to maim, consort with evil spirits, provoke love, or seek buried treasure.

In **1564**, the **Queen** passed an amendment to the Act on her most trusted advisors' advice. **The Dee Sanction** permitted the practice of magick in defence or for the beneficence of the realm. And, it created a loophole through which convicted traitors might use their heretical knowledge to work a penance in service to Her Majesty.

The **Sanction** fell under the jurisdiction of both **Francis Walsingham**—master of the Queen's spy network in Europe—and **Doctor John Dee**—astrologer, alchemist and companion in words to the Queen. They recruited the fortunate malefactors rescued from execution as **Agents**, bound to a covert intelligence service.

The Dee Sanction offered the first line of defence against inimical forces, both common and supernatural.

Dee and Walsingham

1535—Abed in the dorm of a Chelmsford school, a boy awoke from a nightmare. In his tormented sleep, he had found himself lost; alone, abandoned of hope, and suffocated by a cloying dark.

He had felt pursued, prey to an unseen hunter. When the beast's hot breath brushed his neck, a light had flared. A halo of flame surrounded a severed hand, fingers oddly pointed. The middle finger, pale and bloodless; the little finger, blackened as if burnt; the thumb, slick with gore.

Come the light of day, the boy didn't speak; he hardly ate for three days until, while studying Euclid, he recovered his senses. The complexity of the vision haunted him. With absolute certainty, the boy knew this terror guarded hidden secrets. John Dee vowed to decipher its mystery...

While they're both utterly loyal supporters and companions to the **Queen**, **John Dee** and **Francis Walsingham** are poles apart in their outlook and upbringing.

Dee had always questioned the order of the Universe and the entities within it, right from his earliest years. He suffered terrible visions and heard voices in his youth; in learning, he sought to challenge everything, seeking patterns and truths amid chaos.

He studied language, philosophy, geography, geometry, astronomy and, most important of all, mathematics. He allowed his visions and wild theories to guide him, using maths to lend the universe structure. In these moments, he uncovered his own interconnectedness with **Princess Elizabeth's** fate—a connection which she implicitly trusted.

Walsingham was son to William Walsingham, lesser gentry and a barrister of repute. Francis gravitated to the study of law too. As a Protestant, he spent five years in Europe during the reign of **Queen Mary**.

He had an eye for detail and a preternatural sense of personality and people. A diplomat at first, then Member of Parliament, he found his way into intelligence via **William Cecil**. He was insightful and level-headed, prepared to make his point no matter the cost. His attitude might have seemed paranoid to some. Still, **Walsingham's** perceptiveness, remarkable recollection and incredible insight allowed him to second guess the **Queen's** enemies time and again.

In a time of favourites, patronage and pride, both **Walsingham** and **Dee's** connection to the Queen remained constant, even though their sway wavered. For their part, they would serve her in ways beyond other's ken within the Court. And in the face of a continent dominated by Catholicism and a populace afeared of heresy and the corruption of the unknown, **The Dee Sanction** may be the only hope.

True Believers

While magick holds no sway in our contemporary times, the Elizabethan world absolutely believed. Throughout Elizabeth's reign—and by no means confined to that period—personalities in and about the court and country pursued various studies in the art of magick, most for advancing their personal ends and fortunes.

The Queen provided support and patronage to those asserting knowledge of the hermetic and scientific lore's bleeding edge. She voiced her desire to learn the ways of alchemy herself, assuming that any claimant could prove a grasp of the secret techniques themselves. The nation's coffers were empty—debts growing progressively throughout the Queen's reign—so, the possibility of turning base metals into gold held a singular allure.

Respected scholars defended unshakeable belief in the esoteric principles of geometry and maths, angels and demons, relics and artefacts. At the same time, they pursued studying the sciences, emulating and expanding upon the past's great minds' theories and practices.

To the informed, modern audience, the beliefs of Elizabethan scholars might seem ridiculous. However, while playing **The Dee Sanction**, those gathered around the table need to set preconceptions aside. While witches may burn or suffer grave tortures, the great courts of Europe embraced matters both magical and spiritual as a means to an end. The 1564 amendment to the Act of Parliament intended to deal with the threat of witches and magick. Only in pursuit of the safety of the realm were consorting with spirits and magick use acceptable.

Matters of magick run a tightrope fraught with peril and potential.

Brief John Dee Timeline

1527: John Dee born in Tower Ward.

1530s: Safety Lies in Fear: Halley's Comet (1531) heralds the rise in supernatural threat and intolerance of the Old Ways.

1548: Dee meets Gerardus Mercator.

1555: Dee and Elizabeth enter a correspondence that cements their trust.

1556: Dee draws up his plans for a Grand Library and seeks patronage for the task.

1560s: All Along the Watchtowers: Dee advocates magical defences to the Queen in the face of rising threat.

1564: The Dee Sanction appended to the 1563 Act Against Conjurations, Enchantments and Witchcraft; Dee establishes his Grand Library at Mortlake.

1570s: Empire Under Siege: Pope Pius V excommunicates Queen Elizabeth and declares open season on her demise at the hand of any loyal Catholic; Walsingham's covert activities branch from those of Cecil.

1580s: Pursuit of Angels: Dee takes his experiments abroad with his scryer Edward Kelley; Francis Drake (1580) circumnavigates the world; Mortlake sacked in Dee's absence.

1587: Execution of Mary, Queen of Scots (Feb); Drake's raid on Cádiz (April); Walsingham incites Ottoman Empire to harrass Spanish fleet in the Mediterranean.

1588: The Spanish Armada foiled.

1590: The School of Night: Walsingham's death; Dee's decline; Henry Percy secures the mantle as England's Archmage.

1600s: Unsanctioned: Discredited and struggling, Dee seeks the means to regain his influence at court under King James. He resurrects a scheme to find the Philosopher's Stone. Sells Mortlake (1608) and apparently dies the following year.

What is The Dee Sanction?

The Dee Sanction is a traditional tabletop **role playing game (RPG)**, loosely based on historical fact and personalities. In an **RPG**, friends narrate stories together. As a **Player**, you act the part of a specific **Player Character (PC)**—an Agent of Dee—in the story. As **Game Moderator (GM)**, you set the scene, lead the tale, play the part of **Non-Player Characters (NPCs)**, and keep order using the rules herein.

The Dee Sanction core rules offer you a set of simple mechanics to run intriguing investigations and missions set against a backdrop of almost-historical Europe. Stories play to the feel and sense of history rather than clinging to every detail; remember, the game should be entertaining for everyone.

In this version of history, **magick** exists, and with it, the possibility that **angels** talk to those who understand them. However, technology and medicine still reside in the realms of wooden-block printing presses and seeking a balance of the elemental humours.

The **Players** are Agents working under the auspices of the **Dee Sanction** to avert supernatural and magical threats. **Agents** are ordinary people with a tainted history, offered a chance to stay their execution and right past wrongs. When an **Agent** does something threatening to their lives or progress, the **Player** rolls a **Die** to determine the outcome.

The **GM** prepares and presents the hook of the story. They detail the setting, the supporting characters, and the challenges. They fill in the sensory detail and answer questions that might be reasonably asked. The **GM** listens to and works with the **Players** to create an exciting story. The **GM** is not out to win but to maintain order and entertain.

Special Terms

The Dee Sanction includes many specific game terms that may be unfamiliar. The **Glossary of Terms**, on page **67**, should help clarify any uncertainty.

5

What it isn't about...

Historical Pedantry

The **Dee Sanction** isn't about pedantry or historical purism. Play to the themes and the feel—like a TV serial or film based on the period that adds *"based on true events"* rather than sweating the small stuff.

The game takes place in an alternate Europe. This version takes its cues from history; it then mixes in supernatural elements, real magick, skewed conflicts and other fabricated events. Your **Table** has the means to control the setting and adjust the mix, tweaking the balance of history and fiction.

Fun and entertainment should be paramount, not a competition or exam over who knows the most facts about the Tudor court!

Whatever You're Not Into

The point of the game isn't to be anything you're not into. If you don't fancy the politics—byzantine as they were—then run adventures away from the Courts. **Agents** will find their lives manipulated by politics, but they need not live in the thick of it.

If you're used to dungeon crawls, there are plenty of ruins, riddled with relics and befouled with spirits. If you fancy investigations, take the sleuth's path and seek a hidden truth or solve crimes.

As the **GM**, tie your adventures back to the game's theme but don't feel that an RPG set in Tudor times needs to be some grey and dismal simulation. **The Dee Sanction** is a setting where the occult agenda presents a clear and present danger to the throne. The hard swerve from recorded history means that you don't need to tie yourself in knots keeping to strict continuity. Nods and notes to continuity will work without labouring over adherence to canonical events.

Game Preparation

You will need a few essentials to play the game; nothing too hard to get a hold of, and with options to improvise.

Firstly, you need to have someone else to play with; one or more other people will do. The **Players** take the role of an **Agent** of the **Dee Sanction**. Simultaneously, the **GM** leads the tale, sets the scene, plays the supporting characters, and keeps order with the rules provided and a little commonsense.

The whole group—the **Table**—should work to make the game entertaining for everyone. That means sharing the load of pushing the story forward, recording events and recalling them at the start of each session, playing fair, and bringing snacks to share! Don't leave it on the **GM**.

Second, you need some gaming essentials—something to write on and write with, as well as a set of **Dice**.

The sort of **Dice** you need is most of a polyhedral set; that's **Dice** with four, six, eight, ten, and twelve sides. The rules refer to a **Die** with a number and "**d**"—**2d6**—meaning you roll that number of dice, or a simple **D** with a number following—**D8**—that means just roll one of that type.

If you don't have those kinds of dice, a pack of **Playing Cards** with jokers will do.

We Don't Need Another Hero

The **Agents** are not heroes. **Dee** recruits those who had no future, criminals sentenced to be executed to pay for their heretical pursuits.

The Agents of Dee are:

- **Vulnerable** – this is a game where characters can and should die if they do not exercise caution. Sacrifice can be a mighty achievement. It tends to be the thing that sticks with **Players** when remembering games!

- **Expendable** – fast character generation and the existence of a "retinue" in service to **Dee** and **Walsingham** mean that even when on distant quests for the cause, replacements are available!

- **Amateurs** – the Elizabethan court was positively creaking under the weight of individuals claiming expertise in matters for which they possessed little actual skill. **Agents** have expertise but never quite enough. They should come to depend on each other to fill out those gaps.

- **Only slightly supernatural** – all of the characters got mixed up on the periphery of the occult. They're not wizards or necromancers; they're hapless dabblers who know that the supernatural exists but cannot command it. They can stretch to *cantrips*, but don't expect *fireballs*!

- **Criminals** – some people know that the Agents have a criminal past, and they're ready to remind them. At the drop of a word, every Agent could find themselves in a cell awaiting execution.

- **(Death) Marked** – **Dee's** sage advice to **Queen Elizabeth** upon the necessity of a supernatural defence for the realm has saved the **Agents** from execution. They

have witnessed the convicted, creaking on the Tyburn Tree—for a brief moment, the spectre of Death caressed their filthy cheek.

- **"Beneath us..."** – Renaissance Europe has an increasing sense of Us and Them. The small favours and privileges that the commoner once considered their due have been swept away. The nobility both despise and fear the poor and downtrodden.

- **Conflicted** – supernatural horrors might tear you apart, so you should run away. But, if you run away, you'll be hunted down and hanged—if you're lucky. It's a rock or a hard place.

- **Mostly in the dark** – on the other hand, you only know as much as anyone tells you, so maybe those horrors have more to do with your nightmares and imagination. Nothing can be that bad, right?

- **Scapegoats** – if you don't do something about it, you can guarantee the blame sits firmly with you. And there are no authorities you can go to for amnesty. No one will believe you if you start blathering on about the occult and strange creatures from other worlds...

A Short Tudor History

"See our Gloriana, Empress of this island pearl, silken robes of crimson her form in might and glamour frame in testament to her father brave"

— Shakespeare, Gloriana

While not a work of historical fact, gameplay will undoubtedly benefit from some base understanding of the Tudor landscape's common features

The fate and fortunes of nobility, gentry and the church swayed and revolved throughout the period, as the throne shifted between Catholicism and Anglican intent.

Society

When you think of Tudor society, think of rural islands interspersed with slightly larger urban enclaves. These enclaves have an increasing pull over the century, magnets for isolated hopefuls—those with aspirations have the opportunity to dash themselves on the rocks of economic and social reality.

The countryside serves as a bread basket for the cities, both as a source of wealth for the nobility and staples for the table of the professional and merchant class.

Prosperity

By the end of the century, the population roughly doubled from more than 2 million to approximately 4 million. Prosperity didn't follow suit. The poor remained impoverished; indeed, statute materialised over the century to deal with the rising tide of vagrancy and roaming unemployed.

Most towns supported a population of one or two thousand, with regular markets at which locals from all around would come to buy and sell. Trades would congregate on the same streets - something applicable to London, other large cities (like York or Norwich) and the smaller towns.

To Traverse the Realm

Whether going to the market, seeking work or travelling with a purpose, most would go on foot or by horse. Roads were poorly maintained tracks at best, few receiving the maintenance warranted or expected by statute. Carts and carriages were rare, uncomfortable and likely to fall afoul of the variable conditions and maintenance of the road.

Traders favoured rivers and coastal waters; ships and boats carrying raw materials, finished goods, and passengers. Many modern coastal towns and villages would once have supported far greater populations and enjoyed considerable prosperity when trade by water dominated.

Discipline

Correction favoured swift and brutal acts over imprisonment. Easier to flog someone or shove them in the stocks. For more severe punishment, the criminal could expect to be maimed as well—removing fingers, ears, or eyes.

Death by hanging or beheading depended on status—the former for the poor and the latter for the wealthy. Whichever the case, the punishment of serious crime drew a large, boisterous and demanding crowd.

The business of maintaining law and order fell to the likes of the parish constables. Roles without pay, those sworn in by local magistrates would as likely line their own pockets by collecting local taxes as execute the word of the law.

Household

Poor folk lived in simple homes composed of one or two rooms, with minimal furnishing, basic bedding, and tallow lighting. Those of greater substance could afford more space, more comfortable and numerous furnishings, and beeswax candles.

Furnishing generally extended to stools, benches, tables and beds. The rich might stretch to glass in their windows, but most others had shutters and strips of linen soaked in linseed oil.

Most ordinary homes would be smoky, smelly and dark, with some effort to alleviate the squalor through the use of sweet-smelling herbs. Rich or poor, most continued to dump the content of their chamber pots outside, with some favouring cesspits to gather the waste. Without sewers or drains and a tendency for rubbish to end up in the streets, towns and cities had an atmosphere that was hard to ignore.

Health and Welfare

In these conditions, plague and disease could decimate towns' and cities' population (in the very Roman sense of the word). None were immune to the blight of sickness and ill-health—**Queen Elizabeth** herself suffering the disfigurement of smallpox in her survival of the disease.

Medicine relied more on superstition than science, with the study of blood, urine, odours, bumps and the stars all having their place in the practitioners' arsenal.

Doctors were expensive and, in truth, providers of no greater certainty of survival than any other medical practitioner. In their place, barber-surgeons, wise women and herbalists exercised what remedies they could to alleviate suffering and illness.

Warfare and Weapons

The period saw the increasing use and efficiency of firearms over the typical bow and arrow. Hand-to-hand weaponry remained a mainstay of the battlefields, including swords, halberds, daggers, axes, and bill-hooks.

Mercenaries and soldiers returning from war would do so with their arms. A lack of general law enforcement could see an argument escalate all too easily into bloodshed.

On the other hand, that same absence of order meant many men of arms would find work as guards, constables or hunters—of both game and criminals.

Whether in town or travelling on the open road, nowhere was safe—few travelled without at least a blade in their possession. Indeed, some wouldn't think it unusual to travel with the pike that once warded off advancing cavalry!

Becoming Agents of Dee

You define your **Agent** by their ability to survive. Each must eke the most out of their expertise and connections to make progress.

The Dee Sanction measures the Agent's essential facets by their **Resources**.

These three values provide a view of your character's base potential – measured in **Physicall**, **Intellectuall** and **Supernaturall**.

Players generate the value of these three Resources by assigning **six** (6) dice steps. No **Resource** can have fewer than one dice step.

Dice Steps	Resource
One (1)	D4
Two (2)	D6
Three (3)	D8
Four (4)	D10
Five (5)	D12

For example, for an extreme build at character creation, you could assign 1D10 to one Resource, 1D4 to another, and place 1D4 in the third - spending the six steps allotted.

The Three Resources

Physicall

The fragility or heft of the mortal form; a measure of the spectrums of force, manual acuity and targeted violence.

- Resistance to physical harm or hindrance, whether fighting with tooth and knuckle or outrunning pitchfork-wielding aggressors

- Painstaking but thorough finger-tip search or a rapid shuffle through book-shelves or drawers

- Shrugging off toxins, shaking off sickness or driving through sleeplessness

Intellectuall

Structured learning and clarity of thought. The association of wits and lore to build defensible concepts and principles.

- Resistance to propaganda, brow-beating, or the manipulation of the facts; logical handling of obscure lore or puzzles

- Calculated deduction of facts from evidence based on clear principles, unyielding laws and academic certainties

- Overcoming deterioration of thought, the insidious influence of strange science, or obfuscation by manipulated fact

Supernaturall

An attunement to the otherness that surrounds and permeates our world. The anchoring of one's essential existence.

- Resistance to distortion of the senses and the wavering strength of personality brought on by madness and possession

- Gut-instinct; the pull of the Other; sensitivity to the flow of the universe as a road to enlightenment

- Weathering delusion, mesmerism, geas, glamour, mind control and similar attempts to overwhelm or erase the essence of the individual

the Dee Sanction

Name: ROBERT THOMAS (62)

Occupation: CARETAKER (17) or (18)

Home: LAVENHAM (61)

(D8) (D6) (D4) (11)

Intellectuall Physicall Supernaturall

Tradecraft (14)

 System   Kit Vigilance

Magic   Access Conspiracy

Expertise & Abilities

ARCHITECTURE
MINISTRATION (12)
MECHANICS

Fortune

 1

(14)

PROBLEMATA—Enlightenment through the study of the theories and devices of the Ancient Greeks. (20)

Injuries & Afflictions

You can visit or mention **@mrgarland4** on **Twitter** to create a basic character outline.

Hits

 3 (13)

(25)

Affiliations & Contacts (19)

GOODLY SERVANTS OF LIGHT—The Servants value objects and structures as a means to channel the wisdom of the Almighty. Building things is good; through making we find the subtle influence of our Lord.

Mundane Possessions

(60)
SHOVEL
IMPRACTICALLY EMBELLISHED HELMET
LEATHER BELT WITH HOOPS

Armour

 0

Download Blank Character Sheets from:
www.thedeesanction.com

Favours & Esoterica (21)

MISCOUNT— Make someone miscalculate with absolute certainty, once per session.

—— Unravelling (14) ——

Back Story

Agents are shaped by their doom. Once ordinary folk, some fateful meeting with individuals of heretical beliefs led them down a dark path. In the end, they paid for their enlightenment by a black spot upon their soul; they ended up in a dank cell with days to live. Then they got an offer that they couldn't refuse—redemption.

An **Agent's** Back Story consists of crucial events in their recent past. A **Player** rolls (or selects) an option from the tables at the end of this section—their **Occupation** (from either—♣ or ♠), a damning **Association** (♥), and a **Focus** (♦) for their enlightenment.

If drawing for options, pull cards from a **Full Unblooded Deck** until you have a ♥, a ♦, and one of either the ♣ or ♠ suit.

Favours of the Angels

Favours represent the low key magical influence that an **Agent** can exert.

The **Player** selects a **Favour** by rolling a **1d4** (column) and a **1d10** (row) or choosing a card from a **Full Unblooded Deck**.

Favours are **Angelic magick** of the lowest form—influence over the base elemental forces of both mortal and unseen world.

Once per game session, they work automatically unless inhibited or prevented from activating. For example, if the **Agents** have ventured into some other realm, like **Hell** or the **Great Wood**, a **Favour** may not function. The **GM** should rule if a **Favour** fails to fire off and allow the **Player** to use it later when freed from their current constraints.

A **Favour** can achieve a minor effect. The **Player** describes it, and the **GM** judges the outcome in mechanical terms. **Favours** can achieve unlikely effects, but they are always small in scale. A flammable item can smoulder and catch without being close to a flame, but an **Agent** cannot make someone combust!

The **GM** has the final call to decide how powerful an effect the **Agent** can achieve. **Favours** have no specific definition or mechanics. If in doubt, err on the side of less than a **Moment**; no larger than a fist; and, never enough for a **Consequence**.

Abilities

A **Back Story** has a brief **Description** and a choice of **Abilities**. An **Ability** is a general area of knowledge, expertise, or experience.

At character creation, choose **three** of the eight **Abilities** presented across your **Back Story**.

You can take **Abilities** from all parts of your **Back Story** or fewer sources—an **Agent** Courtier could just choose the three from the **Occupation** and ignore the rest. As you survive future missions, you have the chance to add more **Abilities**.

Abilities can be used both passively and actively. In an ordinary and stress-free situation, you can use an **Ability** to explain why your **Agent** can do something, discover something, or know a given fact. You get what you want without a **Resource** roll.

When **Challenged**, an **Agent** with a relevant **Ability** will get a **Step Up** (▲).

Abilities have no specific definition. They all represent a particular area of expertise. Their definitive limits of use fall to negotiation between **GM** and **Player**. Lean toward "useful sometimes" rather than "always helpful," if in doubt.

Hits and Unravelling

An Agent's **Hits** signpost the harm they can withstand. You lose **Hits** when you waver in facing a **Threat** or **Hazard**.

An Agent's personality consists of a balance of humours—illustrated by your **Unravelling**. Fear and the unnatural may lead to your **Agent** displaying uncharacteristic behaviour if you **Falter** (see page **22**).

Agents start with **3 Hits** and **D8 Unravelling**.

Fortune

Each **Player** starts with a single **Fortune** token that they can spend to force the re-roll of any single throw of the **Die** (or **Dice**). **Fortune** refreshes between **Adventures**, not between game sessions.

The **GM** (or the whole **Table**) may choose to reward a **Player** with an extra **Fortune**—say, for excellent roleplay or unexpected heroics.

The **Agents** of Dee are not the luckiest people, but they have other tools and allies to call upon when pressed or in danger.

Take a Chance

Not all tasks align with a specific **Resource**. Sometimes it boils down to pure luck. The toss of a coin, heads or tails—or *the crown or the crosse*, as an Elizabethan coin would bear the sovereign one side and a cross upon the other.

As **GM**, never leave a pivotal clue to chance. If the story stalls for lack of information, you have no one to blame but yourself. Beyond **Resources** and **Abilities**, chance should be the next means to find additional information only if that detail is not apparent.

If you have some element that might arise from knowing a random fact or events that might go either way with no means to influence the outcome, then **Take a Chance**.

Either flip a coin and call it, or roll **1d6** and look for a result **4 or higher**. In that case, they make a connection or events flow favourably. The **GM** will provide any extra detail, and the adventure moves on. Roll **3 or lower** and the outcome **Falters**, not so much as to cripple progress, but certainly not making life any easier.

Optional and Frivolous

Round off **Agent** creation with elements like appearance, clothes, accent, and so forth. The book's appendices (page **60 - 62**) contain random tables to help choose a **name**, a **home** town, an unusual **mannerism**, and a few small, unique **possessions**.

Tradecraft

The Dee Sanction does not select **Agents** on some arbitrary basis. The key to the **Agents'** success lies in their backstories and network of experience.

Neither **Dee** nor **Walsingham** found the **Queen's** trust by chance. Her confidence in them derives from their focus, foresight and fair judge of character. **Agents** have the means to strive toward the truth or pluck an ace from the hole through their combined know-how.

Every **Agent** may not contribute to every **Scene**. Still, collectively the group benefits from their combined history, connections and aptitude.

Tradecraft represents this pool of resource from which **the whole group** will draw. You can see the collected options in a box of icons near the top of the character sheet.

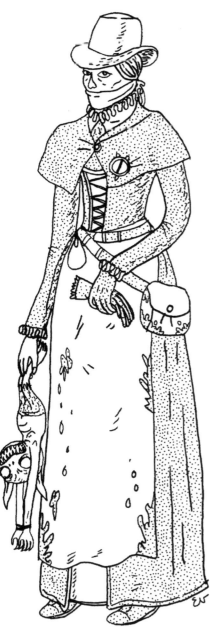

Establishing and Using Tradecraft

The **Team** must choose **one Tradecraft** after being briefed on a mission's nature.

The selection refreshes at the start of each adventure—assuming that the next adventure's focus has a new direction and is not just a continuation of the last session.

Tradecraft has both narrative and mechanical value and has two possible uses. **Agents** can:

- Benefit from the value of the **Tradecraft** as if they possessed a **general Ability** across the whole team; or

- **Deplete** it to cancel or neutralise a **Mark**; Agents might nnot achieve a goal or overcome an adversary without it.

Tradecraft's function as an **Ability** is not retained beyond the adventure. Think of it as a character in an episodic TV series with an interest or hobby that never features again.

Narratively, the **Table** can decide which Agent to associate the **Tradecraft** selection with reference to their past adventures.

*For example, the **Agents** choose **Access** and note that they had expert assistance in animal-handling techniques from a representative of the Guild of Loriers. For this adventure, they can use that to calm, guide, and assess animal wellbeing. Throughout the adventure, one Agent shows a particular affinity for the animals. In later missions, he keeps a reputation as something of a soft touch when dealing with beasts.*

This connection between **Agent** and **Tradecraft** colours their reputation. The **GM** might work that into the story or note it for an ad hoc bonus.

Tradecraft also represents how the **Agents** attempt to prepare for the unexpected and the unknown. Enemies, hazards and events may have one or more **Marks**. To overcome or cancel a **Mark** requires the **Group** decide to deplete—use up—their **Tradecraft**.

*For example, the Grand Wolf of Strathnavern can be tracked and battled but not so simply defeated. To defeat it requires knowledge of the creature's True Name, a seasoned dagger of thrice lightning-struck iron, and a silver-furred wolfskin. To denote this, the profile of the Grand Wolf is marked (**CKM**).*

To defeat a target with more than one **Mark** requires more than one adventure. Indeed, if the **Agents** misjudged the mission, they might have no suitable **Tradecraft** to aid in their first encounter.

*To defeat the Grand Wolf, the Agents need a combination of **Conspiracy** (true name\location), **Kit** (wolfskin), and **Magic** (a hazel-seasoned thrice-lightning-struck iron dagger). Unfortunately, their brief for the first adventure led them to select **Access**; they cannot make progress this mission.*

As a win condition, **Tradecraft** serves to show how the **Agents** have assessed and prepared. As the **GM**, creating a goal or threat with multiple **Marks** increases the difficulty and adds complexity. To win the game, the **Agents** need to engage in additional missions to acquire all the tools and information they need to succeed.

The Agents cannot defeat the Grand Wolf of Strathnavern in one go. In the first adventure, they discover how it might be defeated in the closing reveal, following a fruitless battle against their formidable enemy—or its minions.

*Over the next three adventures, the Agents will need to select **Conspiracy**, **Kit**, and **Magic** as their Tradecraft selections, in whatever order they choose.*

If the **Agents** chose one of the **Tradecraft** needed to defeat a target for the session, they have the chance to advance toward their goal in the first adventure.

*For example, with **Conspiracy**, the Agents discover the Grand Wolf's true name and identity as a benefactor of Mary, Queen of Scots.*

As a narrative tool, gathering the means to achieve a goal forces the **Agents** to make careful choices based on limited information. This might make an Adventure more challenging where that **Tradecraft** doesn't neatly map with their current goal. A wily **GM** might exploit, or at least call out, this dichotomy.

In addition, a **GM** can have lesser hazards and events in an adventure that **Tradecraft** can resolve, but which would lead to early depletion.

*For example, the **Agents** can use **Access** to enter the Tower of London or **Magic** to bribe Emperor Rudolf II with a rare treasure to buy time in the dungeons with Edward Kelley.*

Ways and Means

The icons on the character sheet (or Journal) identify six broad influences in **Tradecraft**, described below (with examples):

 Access (A) summarizes the people, groups, and associations known to the Agents, such as allowing them to strike off a favour owed, acquire temporary use of some rarity or sidestep an awkward situation.

- Bodyguards willing to turn a blind eye
- Little known guilds providing services at the most advantageous moment
- Loan of the tongue of St Anthony

 Conspiracy (C) represents agency and action that questions both the status quo and commonsense. The crumbling hold of the Church and the diverse powerplay across the courts of Europe led to the institution of myriad combines and sodalities. Orders focussed on obscure Biblical tracts, influential personalities, or notions of divine heritage as their central tenet.

- Shadowy personalities and authorities on the fringes of the Court with veiled influence or avenues of admittance

- Ancient orders with obtuse agendas that fund alms and support groups such as to make anyone a potential agent or resource

- Insidious theories perpetuated by mainstream certainty in divine right, ancient pacts or enigmatic events, like the all-too-often prophesied end times

 Kit (K) outlines the Agents' preparedness, possessing the right piece of mundane equipment, clothing, material or ingredient at just the right time. Often, the possession of a critical item ties back to a friend, companion or mentor who insisted on never going anywhere without it.

- Keeping a dagger of cold iron or sanctified silver concealed on your person

- Token of strange provenance prepared in circumstances unique and unrepeatable

- Knowing the location of a secret cache or dropbox known only to members of a specific association, guild or coterie

 Magic (M) frames the Agents' immersion in the periphery of the Other World. Given the attitude across Europe to witchcraft, recognition or confession to a knowledge of magick is tantamount to signing your own death warrant. Contacts will expect complete anonymity and mutual respect for their continued occultation as a source.

- The recollection of forgotten dialects, obscure argot, or cryptic prophecies

- Recent correspondence with incarcerated heretics, condemned witches, and exiled magi of the European courts

- Acquaintance with unfamiliar folklore, occult science, proscribed diaries, or the abstruse theories of the ancient world

 System (S) describes an Agent's familiarity with the pullies and levers required to sidestep the law, accelerate bureaucracy and bulls-eye the loopholes in the monolithic European establishment and officialdom.

- Possession of papers signed by some notable of high standing and unquestionable influence

- Timely and detailed awareness of ancient customs and strange by-laws, or those esoteric orders established in prior times to maintain them

 Vigilance (V) portrays a flair for watchfulness, curiosity and caution. The gift of a well-timed revelation that either puts an adversary off guard or furnishes a colleague with insight.

- Connections into low-level local intelligence gathering about whereabouts, routine or the specific presence of an individual or object

- Having the right person in the right place at precisely the right time

- Inspiration sprung from the possession of all the puzzle pieces or the keystone in a complex conundrum.

Occupation — part I

	Roll/Draw	Description	Abilities
Doctor	A♣ (1)	Assistant to one of the few chartered physicians who claim recognition for their depth of medical knowledge	*Reassurance* *Anatomy* *Diagnosis*
Unperson	2♣	Dweller of the streets, alleyways, lanes, and back roads, surviving hardship through a wealth of wit and wile	*Burglary* *Passage and Path* *Street Smarts*
Friar	3♣	One of the scattered mendicants of a broken order, seeking support and goodwill from the generous and those seeking beneficence	*Begging* *Quote and Verse* *Gourmand*
Barber Surgeon	4♣	No lesser in knowledge than learned doctors, practitioners of skills far and above a simple cut and shave	*Bleeding* *Dentistry* *Astrology*
Painter-Stainer	5♣	Specialists in the decoration, colouring and gilding of buildings, furnishings, and other objects; of a Guild well known for disagreements and violent dispute	*Painting* *Decorate* *Goading*
Courtier	6♣	Watchful and ever mindful attendant on the periphery of the gatherings of Court	*Diplomacy* *Dance* *Connoisseur*
Porter	7♣	Like Atlas with the weight of the world upon their shoulders, they pack and prepare luggage for travellers of all standings	*Observant* *Prepared* *Negotiation*
Scrivener	8♣	Clerk and note-taker, responsible for keeping record of the passage of events and notable deeds for all who can pay for the privilege of paperwork	*Papercraft* *Calligraphy* *Bureaucracy*
Horse Trader	9♣	Trader in all manner of livestock; accused, by reputation, to play the game and perhaps pull the wool over unguarded eyes for a profit	*Intimidation* *Probability* *Animal Welfare*
Clerk of the Temple	10♣	Close associate of those who practice the law, serving with a willing ear, a strong stomach and a tenacious head lock	*By-Laws and Loopholes* *Grappling* *Carousing*

Occupation — part II

	Roll/Draw	Description	Abilities
Minstrel	A♠ (1)	Welcome provider of entertainment, in forms many and varied, in court and drinking holes alike	Song and Story Acrobatics Tomfoolery
Scavenger	2♠	An officer of the ward responsible for managing the handling and removal of domestic waste	Carriage-Handling Scavenging Night Working
Herbalist	3♠	Practitioners in traditional treatments and curatives garnered and prepared from both cultivated gardens or the open commons and woodlands	Comfort Herbalism Brewing
Artist	4♠	Creator of emotive miniatures and decorative illuminations for varied patrons, ideally with deep pockets	Drawing Counterfeit Nostalgia
Waterman	5♠	Lewd-mouthed punters upon freshwater courses able to chart a safe course through accreted silt, discarded rubbish, and narrow channels	Gossip Navigation Boating
Gardener	6♠	Hard-working keepers of small plots, in town and country, for flowers, vegetables and simples	Foraging Labouring Beekeeping
Caretaker	7♠	Trusted keeper of buildings and wider properties, notably in the absence of the master of the house	Cooking Farming Hunting
Official of the Watch	8♠	Thankless volunteer keepers of order tasked with bringing the wretched and the immoral to justice	Forgery Gambling Apprehend
Messenger	9♠	Second-fiddle diplomats burdened with the drudgery of carrying letters, papers, and commodious gratuities	Rumour Orienteering Traversing
Craftsperson (Specify type)	10♠	Apprenticed specialist disciplined in the adept working of raw materials into products of saleable value	Barter Materials (Craft-specific) Reworking

Association	Roll/Draw	Description	Abilities
Goodly Servants of Light	A♥ (1)	Belief in the prophetic focus served in the construction and scrutiny of monuments as a means to channel the wisdom of the Almighty	Architecture Orienteering Ministration
Star of Artemis	2♥	Religion stems from layers of deceit; true faith has been mired in ancient propaganda	Mythology Archaeology Flattery
Pythagorean Brotherhood	3♥	Believers that understanding lies in the intersection 'tween number and form	Numerology Geometry Debate
The Octagon Society	4♥	Splinter of the Knights Templar with a focus on attaining a balance in both mind and spirit as a route to a higher purpose or form	Phrenology Meditation Sleight-of-Hand
Chevaliers des Trois Imposteurs	5♥	Fractious movement intent on bringing about Enlightenment in an Age of False Religions	Antiquity Commerce Eloquence
Druids of the Eternal Grove	6♥	Ancient order seeking to revive the Druidic faith of Celtic legend and restore balance to the world	Natural History Folklore Quieten the Common Beast
Compagnonnage	7♥	Frustrated upstart craftfolk intent on bringing about a new order to unseat the Guilds and wider society	Hand Crafting Devices Bargaining
Orbus Tertius	8♥	Committed to gathering evidence of a hidden realm of perception that will allow transcendence to Mastery	Influence Petty Theft Herbology
Society of Jesus	9♥	Jesuit infiltrators intent on overthrowing the Queen and the Church of England	Infiltration Anthropology Dyeing
Brothers of the Rose	10♥	Believers in esoteric truths of the past, seeking insight into nature, the universe and the spiritual realms	Politics Concealment Provocation

Focus	Roll/Draw	Description	Abilities
Rites of Eleusis	A ◆ (1)	Cryptic insights into higher wisdom scattered in fragments across many minor works, the progression through which one might achieve transcendence	Brewing Organisation
The Voynich Manuscript	2 ◆	Impenetrable occult catalogue, filled with an unknown alphabet; peppered with strange imagery, understanding demands time and focus	Astrology Recreation
Liber Salomonis	3 ◆	Ceremonial traditions incorporating the distilled wisdom of King Solomon, with particular attention to discourse with spiritkind	Purification Detect Lies
Steganographia	4 ◆	Cryptographic guide hidden within a text on symbolic and ancient languages used for discourse with spirits and demons	Signs Ciphers
De Neycomancia	5 ◆	Philosophy and practise upon the invocation of the dead and entities bound to the spirit realm	Clairsentience Mediumship
De Principibus et Regibus Daemoniorum	6 ◆	Cryptic discourse on the theory and notional key in the identification and naming of daemons, devils and dark fae	Names Deception
Problemata	7 ◆	Annotated and dissected record of the mechanisms and devices constructed (or even theorised) by the Ancient Greeks	Construction Mechanics
Das Buch der Nacht	8 ◆	Scrawled diaries of a Grand Wizard who purports to have discovered the Truth at the heart of the Universe	Occult Lore Navigation
The Sins of Longinus	9 ◆	Discourse on the medieval legend around the final days of the Christ	Blacksmithery Theology
The Hollow Hills	10 ◆	Theories and legends upon an inner world of lost people and forgotten knowledge	Astronomy Climbing

	♠	♦	♣	♥
A	**BREATH** MEASURED, STEADY, CONTROLLED, HELD	**SCENT** CURIOUS, UNEXPECTED, CONFUSING, FRESHEN	**WHISPER** CONFIDENTIAL, HISSING MISHEARD, UNHEARD	**GASP** DESPERATE, SUDDEN, SHARP EXHALATION
2	**SPARK** FLASH, SUDDEN, SPIT, STAB, PINPOINT	**START** EXCITE, ROUSE, DROP	**CLAP** ROAR, RUMBLE, CRASH, DISTRACT, FLINCH	**DISQUIET** BOTCH, DISTRUST, UNSETTLE
3	**SCORCH** BURN, SEAR, CHAR	**CATCH** INFLAME, KINDLE, SMOKE	**SKIP** EXCITED, LEAPING	**BLISTER** DEGRADE, BUBBLE, SCALD, IRRITATE
4	**PULSE** DISTURB, VIBRATE, RIPPLE	**THUMP** SHOCK, BRUISE, SLAP, PULP	**CREAK** SCARE, DISTRACT, WORRY, DETOUR	**BAFFLE** MYSTIFY, ANNOY, CONFUSE, DISTRACT
5	**DECAY** NECROSIS, NUMBNESS, TO DUST, LIQUIFY	**SNAP** WEAKEN, ABRADE, CRIPPLE	**TAINT** CLOUD, TOXIFY, DISCOLOUR	**CORRODE** DISCOLOUR, DULLED, BRITTLE
6	**DRIP** TRICKLE, LEAK, PERPLEX	**POOL** GATHER, COALESCE, SLIDE, SPLOSH	**CHOKE** GASP, CLOG, STIFLE, GAG	**MOISTEN** STAIN, SPATTER, DAMP
7	**CHILL** SHIVER, PRESERVE, COOL, NUMB	**FLURRY** CLOAK, SMOTHER, BLIND	**FROST** SLIDE, SLIP, OBSCURE	**SHIVER** SHUDDER, SHIMMY, UNEASY, SHRIVEL
8	**DIRT** GATHER, SINK, PILE, MOLEHILL, POTHOLE	**BLOOM** REVIVE, FLOWER, SCENT THICKEN	**TRAIL** TRACKS, MUDDY, MIRE, DISTORT	**ROT** SPOIL, STINK, MOULD, WEAKEN
9	**GLARE** BLAZE, BLIND, REFLECT	**GLIMMER** ATTRACT, DISTRACT, SCINTILLATE	**TWILIT** GLOOM, LONG SHADOW, VAGUE, DIMSIGHT	**SIGNAL** WARN, COMMUNE, AWAKEN, FLARE
10	**SHADOW** CONCEAL, LURK, VEIL	**OVERLOOK** BLINDSIDE, MISCOUNT, OMIT	**BENIGHT** DARKEN, ENGULF, OVERCAST	**GLOWER** BROOD, NIGHTMARE, EVIL-EYE

The Heart of the Game

Role-playing games involve a lot of story-telling, but everything isn't merely made up. If played totally on the fly, you would soon descend into an argument.

To prevent chaos, the **GM** keeps order by applying the rules outlined in this game section. Broadly, but not strictly, the rest of this core book is intended for a **GM's** use only.

Players explain what they want their Agent to do, how they plan to do it, and what effort or preparation they apply to make the outcome more achievable. The **GM** has the job of interpreting the proposed action, explaining the price of failure, and using the game mechanics to define the challenge.

Sometimes that will mean a throw of the dice; other times, the stated activity just plays out. Either way, the story moves along.

Only the **Players** roll dice to resolve a **Challenge**. If they fail—or **Falter**—the **Player** can expect their **Agent** to suffer for progression.

Challenges

When success or failure comes into question, you have a **Challenge**. The **Player** explains their intent and what the **Agent** does to achieve it. The **GM** then:

1. States the potential positive/negative outcome of an action (**Consequences**);

2. Names the **Resource** involved;

3. Calculates any **Advantage** or **Disadvantage** that applies to the roll.

The **Player** rolls the **Die** associated with the stated **Resource**—**Physicall**, **Intellectuall**, or **Supernaturall** (abbreviated as **Phy**, **Int**, or **Sup Ch.**) to meet the **Challenge**.

If the result is a **1 or 2**, then that **Challenge Falters**; the **Agent** suffers some form of **Consequence**. This is not an outright loss but called failing forward; the **Agent** makes progress, but with adverse complications.

In a fight, a **Falter** usually means suffering harm in the form of a **Hit** and/or some form of **Consequence** (see **Fighting**). For any other **Challenge**, a **Falter** means achieving the desired effect in a way that complicates things—maybe something breaks or clatters.

Any other result on the **Die** means **Success**; the **Agent** achieves the intended outcome.

Step-Up and Step-Down

The **GM** may increase or ease a **Challenge's** difficulty because of factors like environment, preparation, or enemy potency.

*For example, an **Agent** with a proper set of lockpicks will find the task of picking a lock easier.*

In this case, you can **Step-Up** (▲) the **Resource**. Assume a **Resource** one higher— a **D6** becomes a **D8**. The maximum is **D12**.

In some situations, the **GM** may judge that the circumstances, conditions, or lack of equipment work against you; then you have to **Step-Down** (▼). You roll the **Resource** as if one (or more) lower on the scale—a **D6** becomes a **D4**.

A drop below **D4** means a **Challenge** becomes a **Call to Fail**. The **GM** asks the **Player** if they choose to drop out or take the pain for the cause. In a fight, the **Agent** may stick at it to draw an enemy's attacks.

Without a suitable **Ability**—a **Lack of Expertise**—the **GM** may judge a task as impossible. Raw **Resources** alone will not meet a **Challenge** requiring knowledge or skill.

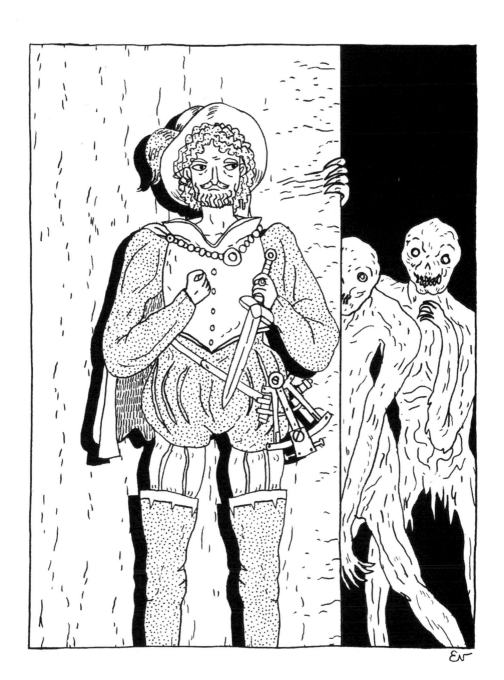

Threats

The **GM** should present any **Challenge** with an adequate explanation of both the up and the downside of facing it. A **Threat** is anything the **GM** uses against the PCs that might hurt or hinder them. That could mean a rampaging cultist twisted by magick, a rabble of booze-bribed soldiers come to rough them up, or a concealed trap.

When Agents face a **Threat**, the **GM** presents it as a **Challenge**. Unlike a standard **Challenge**, **Threats** intend to cause harm by inflicting loss of **Hits** and/or **Consequences**.

An **Agent** with no **Resource** to face the **Threat**—due to a **Step-Down** below D4—will always come off worse from a fight. It would be better to fall back and return later, prepared and with reinforcements.

The Order of Bloodshed

A fight continues until one side expires, surrenders or runs away. A **Moment**—roughly a dozen seconds of activity—breaks down into four stages.

1. Check Initiative
2. State Goal
3. Resolve Attacks (initiative order)
4. Handle Damage

Check Initiative

At the start of each **Moment**, determine initiative by **Taking A Chance**. **Agents** make the check as a group, though the **GM** may need to handle exceptions.

On a **Falter**, all of the enemies will act first. Otherwise, the **Agents** all act first.

The Agents should re-check the order of initiative at the start of each **Moment**.

State Goal

Each character—whether **Player** or **GM** controlled—states their **Goal** for that **Moment**. A **Goal** should be something simple and break down into one or two acts—like "*I move past the guard and snatch the keys*" or "*I slip beneath my enemy's defences and swing upward with my sword.*"

A **Goal** likely has an "**AND**" in it unless an Agent wants to focus on one thing. In that case, they can perform that act with greater magnitude, intensity or concentration. A **Player** who says, "I run as fast as I can", will move at least twice as far as someone who moves and does something else.

The **GM** has the final say on judging the practicality of a **Goal**.

Resolve Attacks

The resolution of all attacks—whether by or upon an **Agent**—is usually resolved with a **Physicall Challenge**. The GM should adjust the Challenge based on circumstance, environment and the adversary's **Potency**. A **Player** rolls to both attack and to defend.

Success—Attack: The Agent deals **Damage** to their opponent. Usually **1 Hit**, the weapon used may cause more or add **Consequences**.

Defend: The character avoids any harm.

Falter—The **GM** throws for **Hit Resolution** to determine the harm or **Consequences** inflicted.

An enemy can attack—forcing a **Challenge** to **Defend**—as many times as its **Attack** value—one unless otherwise stated. All other enemy damage comes from responses to failed attacks by the **Agents**.

The **GM** is free to choose the target of an enemy's attacks.

All or Nothing Defense

Instead of attacking, an **Agent** can choose solely to **Defend**. They **Step-Up** their **Physicall Resource** to roll the **Challenge**. If they succeed, they avoid damage from their opponent and one other attack in the current **Moment**. Otherwise, they sustain an injury as usual.

Fighting Unarmed

Attacking someone without a weapon or intent to disable is achieved by only inflicting **Consequences**. Wrestling might impose a **Restrained** condition while smacking someone with a billy-club could render them **Dull-Headed**.

If someone has **Consequences** sufficient to no longer roll a specific **Resource**, they're considered subdued or rendered harmless. Subdued **NPCs** can no longer resist or fight.

Handling Damage

Hits measure your capacity to soak up hurt and harm. When you lose all **Hits**, you're put **Out of Action**.

At **0 Hits**, you're dying, but your life might yet be salvaged. A cruel or mindless foe could end you unless a colleague steps in to defend you; a **GM** should invite the opportunity for such a response.

Resistance

Armour or other forms of protection provides **Resistance** that negates Hits suffered from an enemy's attacks.

If someone strikes an **armoured** target, roll the die indicated. A result of **1 or 2** negates any **Hits** suffered unless noted otherwise.

Out of Action

At **0 Hits**, an **Agent** is dying. Without assistance, they will expire. Every **Moment**, after reaching **0 Hits**, the **Player** must **Take a Chance** and note each **Falter** (in the two boxes beneath an Agent's **Hits**). When they **Falter** for the third time, the **Agent** dies.

If another character spends a **Moment** to offer aid, a successful **Intellectuall Challenge** will **Stabilize** the dying **Agent**. If the check **Falters**, the dying **Agent** must immediately **Take a Chance** again. The aid-giver can administer additional support, if they choose, during a later **Moment**.

Once stable:

- the **Agent** has **0 Hits** but isn't dying;
- the **Player** rolls on the **Out of Action** table—and the **GM** chooses an appropriate **Consequence** from the outcome.

D6	OUT OF ACTION
1	**Stunned**: Numb, Raving
2	**Senseless**: Dazed, Fat-headed
3	**Fragile**: Shaking, Exhausted
4	**Overcome**: Mute, Humiliated
5	**Wasted**: Unguarded, Fearful
6	**Blood-soaked**: Gory, Oozing

The business of dying won't start again unless they suffer further harm. A **Player** cannot remove **Falter** marks accrued from their **Take a Chance** roll until their **Agent** has a chance to rest—outside of the current **Scene**.

Rest and Recuperation

Agents must have the equivalent of a full night's rest (i.e. 6–8 hours) to recover all **Hits**.

Otherwise, they recover a **Single Hit** for every two hours of uninterrupted sleep.

Consequences

Many attacks and hazards inflict **Consequences** in addition to **Hits**. Some **Consequences** linger, like **Poisoned** or **Paralyzed**. Others are temporary and resolved in a **Moment**, like standing up to negate a **Fallen** state or making distance to break being **Flanked** by overwhelming opposition.

An **Agent** may need to seek specialist assistance to remove a lingering **Consequence**— like finding an apothecary to neutralise a **Poison** or a doctor to mend a **Broken Arm**.

- A lingering Physicall **Consequence** is called an **Injury**, like a **Sprained Wrist** or **Internal Bruising**;

- A lingering Intellectuall or Supernaturall **Consequence** is called an **Affliction**, like becoming **Baffled** or **Haunted**.

- A situational **Consequence** impacts one or more **Resources**. It is temporary—like a **Fallen** Agent or one **Flanked** by foes.

The **GM** should invoke a **Consequence** as the basis for a **Resource** to **Step-Down** as part of a **Challenge**. On the same grounds, an **Agent** can gain the advantage of a **Step-Up** where a **Consequence** impacts an enemy—like **Agents** who manage to **Flank** a monster or fight a foe **Mired** in deep water.

The **GM** can state that a **Consequence** makes a **Challenge** impossible. For example, an Agent cannot sprint with a **Twisted Ankle**.

If an **Agent** sustains three identical lingering **Consequences**, the GM can cancel all but one and inflict a **Hit**. So, an **Agent** with three instances of **Bleeding**, would scratch two and be **Bleeding** and take a **Hit** in harm.

The Nature of the Enemy

You can specify antagonists in a few values:

Name – common name or nickname

Hits – the number of **Hits** required to defeat a **Threat**; at 0 **Hits**, an antagonist is **Out of Action** and unable to contribute meaningfully to the ongoing conflict, i.e. unconscious, lolling listlessly, or dying.

Resistance – type and strength of the antagonist's defences, dice thrown to avoid harm, and any **Tradecraft** required to defeat them with finality. The format:

$$(\blacktriangledown or \blacktriangle \#, \#d\#, ACKMSV)$$

represents **potency**, **armour** and **Tradecraft**. For example:

$$(\blacktriangle 2, 1d4, ACKMSV)$$

It could be a slow-moving **elemental giant**— easy to hit but fiendishly hard to harm or defeat. A capable unarmoured commoner might show as:

$$(None)$$

Indicating no **potency** or **Tradecraft** adjustment, with no **armour**.

Potency: apply a **Step-Down** (e.g. $\blacktriangledown$1) or **Step-Up** (e.g. $\blacktriangle$1) to an **Agents** roll to attack or defend—it might be any value from $\blacktriangle$2 through to $\blacktriangledown$6. The **GM** may rule **Agents** can reduce the impact of a enemy's **Potency** through **Consequences**, like **Flanked**.

Armour: when an **Agent** strikes an enemy, roll the indicated die. A result of 1 or 2 resists the Hit. The **armour** is **Physicall** unless marked—for example, **1d8 Mg** means protection from both magical and common attacks. Special armour will include additional detail under **Abilities**.

26

Tradecraft: a letter indicates a specific requirement for defeat. If the Agents do not have those required items or preparation, they can only achieve a stalemate.

An enemy's **Abilities** will list any specifics, but a letter can just be shorthand for any suitable preparation. **M** might mean using a **Magical** weapon or performing a ritual to deliver the killing blow. In the meantime, a **K** just requires the use of specialised **Kit**.

Hit Resolution – harm an enemy inflicts when an Agent **Falters** their combat **Challenge**. Some options have extra variables— notably **Consequences**—or might change as the battle progresses. The default is:

- ♥ [1,2] **Back Off**: 0 Hits; make distance
- ♣ [3,4] **Jab**: 0 Hits, **Bruised**
- ♦ [5,6] **Graze**: 0 Hit, **Bloody**
- ♠ [7,8] **Solid Strike**: 1 Hit

Make distance means forfeiting the opportunity to strike to move away. An enemy overwhelmed or **Flanked** by **Agents** will end any **Consequence** suffered and might flee depending on circumstance or **Reaction**.

When an enemy **Attacks**, the GM can target any **Agent** in range and force a **Challenge** to **Defend**, adjusted by **Potency** as usual. **Success** avoids harm; a **Falter** causes a roll of **1d6+2** on the **Hit Resolution** table (or remove the ♥ from the draw).

Abilities – usually, this spot contains any other details about the potential the individual or entity has to cause harm, complication or run amok. If the threat has more than one attack, it will be listed here as **Attacks**: #.

As noted, some threats will have vulnerabilities that can only be exposed through the expenditure of **Tradecraft**. Knowing that

the **Grand Wolf of Strathnavern** can only be genuinely defeated with a combination of **Magic**, **Conspiracy** and **Kit** means that a straight battle can only end in a stalemate.

Here's a succinct threat:

Off-Duty Soldier, 2 Hits (none)

The **Off-Duty Soldier** can take two harm and deliver a **Solid Strike**, at best, if the **Agent** falters in their attack.

The enemy has no special resistance. **2 Hits** of damage will render the enemy helpless. An **Agent** could take this opponent down quickly.

As a more complex opponent, heretics in the deep country of Europe might be represented with the notation below:

Angry Mob – 1d4+2 Hits (1d8)

- ♥ [1,2] **Run Away**: 0 Hits; roll **1d12** minus harm sustained; if **Falter**, break and run
- ♣ [3,4] **Confuse**: 0 Hits; **Dizzy**
- ♦ [5,6] **Overrun**: 1 Hit; **Phy Ch.**, **Falter: Fallen**
- ♠ [7,8] **Rally**: 1 Hit; recover 1 Hit (4 people)

Overwhelm: The mob consists of 4 x Hits people; it inflicts half its Hits (rnd up) in automatic harm per Moment. Choose random Agents equal to the potential harm and inflict 1 Hit to each.

The mob is a bustling, frantic gathering of enemies. Half the time it's milling around considering whether to run away or not. The rest of the time it's poking with pitchforks, jostling and shoving. **Overwhelm** means the **Mob** can cause damage even if the **Agents** don't miss a beat.

An average Agent would struggle to handle a Mob without assistance or good fortune.

You can find diverse and varied adversaries in **Appendix D: Bestiary** (page **63–66**).

The Unravelling

The power of faith is real and struggling. **Catholicism** came under fire for, and **Protestant** reform called into question, the belief in the manifestation of sanctity—the body of Christ at communion, the earthly influence of saints, holy places, the power of the crucifix. **Henry VIII** continued to believe, but the monasteries' Dissolution ravaged the earthly symbols of belief, and it snapped a thread and set the **Unravelling** in motion.

The dense and trackless forest, the shadowy stretches of rambling roads, the ruins of sacked churches—the otherworldly slithered through widening gaps in the weave of our world. Once folklore found power as a tool of education and warning; now it became something visceral and dangerous.

The return of the supernatural brought with it primaeval power that might reshape the world. Chaos erupts in dark places, and the **Wild Hunt** rides out. The oldest, strongest emotion of mankind is fear, and the oldest and strongest kind of fear is fear of the unknown.

Unravelling measures these changes' effect upon ordinary people, like the **Agents**. Exposure to unnatural horrors, unbridled chaos, and the influence of other worlds disrupts their delicate psyche.

Trauma manifests as bursts of inconsistent behaviour that twist and strain personality and relationships. Like a thread twisted and pulled to breaking point, an **Agent** can suffer unsettling and disturbing drifts when exposed to the inhuman, the abhorrent, and the impossible.

Handling the Unravelling

When an **Agent** confronts inhuman horror or the supernatural, roll their **Unravelling Die**. If the roll **Falters**, then the die steps down.

When the **Unravelling Die** drops, the **Agent** experiences a temporary shift in their humours—the equilibrium of elements that shapes their personality and wellbeing. Roll both a **1d8** and **1d6** (or make a deck of four cards—one of each suit—then draw one, then one of the rest) and consult the outcome on the **Humours** table (next page).

The **Immediate Effect** (the **1d8**) persists as indicated or for the rest of the **Scene**. The **Ongoing Consequence** (the **1d6**) lasts until the **Agent** has a chance for a long rest, like overnight sleep.

If dropped below **D4**, **Unravelling** works like a **Call to Fail**. If the **Agent** cannot avoid the source of the roll, they automatically **Falter**.

Unravelling cannot recover without rest or professional intervention (like a doctor). A night of rest will restore one lost **Die**. A week of rest is required to recover any further loss.

The Strongest Kind of Fear

The **GM** may judge an experience as more or less frightening, depending on the situation, how personal the experience might be, and the measure of weird.

In deeply personal or incomprehensible situations, **Step Down** the Die before rolling. A minor fright or discovery may **Step Up** the Die or not justify any roll at all.

Humour

D8 — **Immediate Effect**

♥ 1,2 Phlegm

Immediate response is dulled senses; acts of **perception** or **problem-solving** are ▼1 while in the presence of fear source.

♣ 3,4 Black Bile

Overwhelmed by extreme emotion. Eyes fill with tears, body wracked by sobbing. **Take a Chance** to complete any complex action in the presence of fear source.

♦ 5,6 Yellow Bile

Character fills with bitter rage toward all allies while in the presence of fear source. **Take a Chance**, act in a selfish way on a **falter**. Attitude persists in the presence of fear source.

♠ 7,8 Blood

Inadvisably optimistic despite the horrors or the difficult situation faced. Blindly positive. Acts of **violence** or **aggression** are ▼1 while in the presence of fear source.

Ongoing Consequences (until next rest)

D6

♣ 1,2 **Fat-witted** – acts carelessly, lacking in reason when making decisions

♦ 3,4 **Canker-sorrowed** – afflicted with a sense of grief, struggling to see worth in self

♠ 5,6 **Unheedy** – lacking in caution and careless of the consequences from any decisions made

♥ 1,2 **Sullen** – resentful silence, overcast with notes of despondency about any situation

♠ 3,4 **Afeared** – prone to tip into panic and alarm at the smallest trigger

♦ 5,6 **Sickly** – trembling with an unshakeable chill; pale and drawn

♣ 1,2 **Crabbed** – prone to sharp changes in emotional state; short-tempered, sharp, and loud

♥ 3,4 **Choleric** – eager for conflict, with a simmering hostility toward everyone and everything

♠ 5,6 **Despiteful** – unforgiving and driven to seek redress for any slight or wrong

♥ 1,2 **Foolish** – recklessly courageous and bold, heedless of the potency or peril of a challenge

♣ 3,4 **Gullible** – willing to believe or trust anyone without adequate evidence

♦ 5,6 **Capricious** – given to sudden, unpredictable, and erratic change in focus

Tools of Arch Defence

"Oh, glowing orb reveal thy truths beyond the pale."

—*Shakespeare, Hermes Thrice and Thrice Again*

In perfect opposition to the **Queen's** enemies that range against her loyal subjects, the Dee Sanction's tools are few. At least, that's the basic principle from the outset.

Throughout the game, the **Agents** will have the opportunity to gather tools, expand their network and hone their **Tradecraft**, but that takes time. The ongoing campaign should offer exciting opportunities to expand the toolset. The basics outlined below provide a baseline of core tools.

The Black Seal / Amulets

Availability: *Commonly carried by all Agents*

Devised by Dee in the 1560s, the Black Seal provides Agents with a means to communicate through a corrupt and incomplete version of the angelic tongue.

In the early days of the Sanction, that mechanism works less effectively because Dee himself had a weak grasp of the concepts. By the 1580s, it can handle all languages.

Dee's original is composed of sanctified wax, cast in a mould of pure gold. The Queen has the mould secured in absolute secrecy.

- Possession allows the wearer to speak and understand all languages

- Those who speak by the Black Seal do so with a neutral timbre, complicating deceit.

- The Seal provides a means to communicate with Dee from a distance (like a pager).

Rumour hints that he can overhear through the device at leisure

The Hieroglyphic Monad

Availability: *Known by all Agents, used to invoke their Favours.*

The Hieroglyphic Monad is an arcane conflation of symbology—esoteric, celestial, astronomical and geometrical—that supports both a standardised approach to ritual and a dependable, if weak, focus for subtle magick.

An Agent can recreate the Monad with a gesture—by staring monocularly through a ringed forefinger and thumb with digits extended, steadied atop an upturned Sign of the Horns—but the spontaneity robs the motif of potency.

- Agents conjure angelic favour through concentration and use of this gesture

- Every sign is grounded in old lore and folk religion; there's always going to be someone who knows what you're doing

- Development of understanding of minor variation in the Monad may unlock alternate effects

The Stone Houses

Availability: *Locations provided to Agents on a need-to-know basis.*

The network of safe houses dot significant European and the Middle Eastern cities—and a couple in the Atlantic colonies. They share one thing in common—the use of mortar, laced with dust from the London Stone, to seal the main door's lintel.

Dee claims this ancient protection is born of Arthurian myth; it seals these properties against malevolence. However, this occult aegis has never been tested to its limits. The Stone Houses are not gifted with anything more than sparse supplies.

- Those wearing the Black Seal may enter the Stone House, but others must be invited to cross the threshold

- The pantries and storerooms of each Stone House offer the basic tools and rations akin to a ship upon a lengthy voyage

- The potency of the dust in the blessed mortar depletes, necessitating periodic repointing

Mercator's Void

Availability: *Never made directly accessible to Agents; held at Mortlake until it went missing after the sacking of the Great Library.*

Following his meeting with Gerardus Mercator in 1548 and the Paradoxical compass's development in the early 1550s, Dee created the Void—a perfect black sphere on a stationary mount.

Used as part of a scrying ritual—instead of the more traditional shewstone—it provides the means, with some degree of success, to divine the general location of persons and objects.

The Void appears to rely on astral associations or links that may become confused—or cast askew—during certain astrological events.

- There's always the possibility that that which is sought may, in turn, perceive those that would seek it

- Astrological, planetary and mathematical alignment improve focus—it's best to seek anything when the stars are right

- Staring into the Void can cause synaesthetic hallucinations

Mister Garland

Availability: *Dee or Walsingham will deploy Mister Garland where Agent briefing requires. Especially suited to any remote activity or Agent activation that's unexpectedly triggered.*

Garland is a supernatural manifestation, like a ghost or one of Kelley's archangels. A comparison in contemporary media might be **Al** from *Quantum Leap* or *Red Dwarf*'s **Rimmer**. Like a mobile phone, Garland may suffer **signal problems** from strong magick or esoteric interference.

Garland serves as briefing officer and communications relay for the **Dee Sanction**. Agents have more contact with Garland than Dee or Walsingham, except during the **Pursuit of Angels** period when Dee and Kelley are close at hand.

The other comparison would be the miniature tape recorder from *Mission: Impossible*, as Garland will provide a mostly one-way **mission briefing**, note any cache of kit, then promptly disappear—often at the moment of an unexpected distraction.

- Assumes the most average appearance, unrestricted by gender, age, race or other physical measures

- Engages with the actions and gestures of direct physical activity, without ever really touching anything

- Possesses the most angelic singing voice with astonishing range and clarity

Enemies of Elizabeth

"Alone, amid a sea of bastards."

—*Shakespeare, Henry III (Part One)*

In seeking a divorce, **King Henry VIII** took lofty matters of faith and stateship into his own hands and severed ties with the Church of Rome. In the Church's eyes and those of loyal Catholics, his divorce from Catherine of Aragon held no sanction in holy law. In turn, his daughter, **Elizabeth**, had no right to the throne.

The challenge of **The Dee Sanction** often arises because Queen Elizabeth has more enemies than friends. You can assume that this is the default state for a one-shot—mistrust everyone and act with caution.

The enemies listed represent a sample of the significant antagonists on the world stage. On the other hand, the **Bestiary** outlines those adversaries of a direct and visceral nature As **GM**, you may array cells, sects, cults, and other factions against the Agents as adversaries. These may, in turn, link to and seek to further the plans of the higher powers.

Each enemy state provides an outline of their purpose and form, notably through their leader's lense. The bullets beneath outline key features of their people and their motivations to help the **GM** consistently colour the Agents' interactions.

Propaganda

Catholics perceive Queen Elizabeth and her authority on an extended-spectrum from indifference to the bastard child of an unsanctioned marriage. By the 1570s, the Pope sought to push toward the latter.

However, in this period, communication and the spread of news depends heavily on the network of traders, travellers and the dispersion of common rumour and gossip.

Unless stated with certainty, the **GM** should roll **1D10** when Agents enter any community capital or seaports to determine how fresh the news is. Outside large urban areas, adjust the roll by **+2**.

D10	FACTUAL LATENCY
1	**Current**: yesterday or today
2 - 3	**Recent**: in last week or three
4 - 7	**Dated**: nothing for months
8+	**Oblivious**: Emperor who?

The Pope & the Catholic Church

In the ancient heart of empires, the Catholic Church's Popes abide in despotic certainty of their singular role as God's hand on Earth. Yet, that hand now quivers with a palsy born of new learning. Publication and broader dissemination of the **95 Theses** were neither the beginning nor end of this. Still, it was a nail in the coffin of Papal omniscience.

Come 1570, **Pope Pius V** declares Queen Elizabeth a heretic. The Church pulls strings upon many puppet states and dutiful nobles before and after this event.

- Assume heresy before faith without reservation, no matter the status or standing

- Insidious constancy of faith makes soldiers, spies and executioners of everyone

- Recover and weaponize the idols and relics lost to apostates, despots and sinners

Mary, Queen of Scots

In place of **Henry VIII's** bastard child, the Catholics would see **Elizabeth's** distant cousin Mary as the rightful heir to the throne. A strange desolation seemed to follow in Mary's wake throughout her life — from her father dying six days after her birth to her husbands' short life expectancy. She enjoyed a fascination and loyalty, not unlike Elizabeth. Yet, her fate was mired in the intrigues and machinations of men.

- Words have unimaginable power; the artifice of manipulating and presenting them lies at the heart of the Stuart armoury

- Distraction, deception and dissimulation; power is secured through the credulity and arrogance of the enemy

- Never give up, never surrender

Rudolf II's Holy Roman Empire

A shadow of the glory of a half-forgotten past, the central states of Europe raised up an Emperor, and that emperor would seek to raise the dead. Faced with the **Ottoman Threat** in the south and unruly nobility across the continent, **Rudolf II** colludes with alchemists and sorcerers to pursue eternal power—and, more ambitiously, eternal life. The Emperor's Court travels, and his collections go with it, including a whole library of books, relics of the Church, artefacts of the ancient world, and a strange menagerie of clockwork creations.

- Gather up the treasures and artefacts of legend. Accept. Coerce. Bargain. Steal. Interrogate. Imprison

- Uncover the secrets of life and death, good and evil, base matter and miraculous potency

- Travel the realm, flagrantly displaying the prizes of the Imperial hoard as both proof of power and a lure for the wise or greedy

King Philip II & the Spanish

Philip II exerts singular power as a ruler, his influence almost omnipresent across the European—indeed, the world—stage. Ruling from within the terrifying, monolithic walls of **El Escorial**, Philip masterminds a thriving, world-grasping empire to rival any other. He possesses both the power and might to ask for anything and ignore everyone.

Rarely seen in public, the King exercises a network that secures both influence and information, waging war when the sword proves the only option. From the hidden depths of El Escorial come both the monks' prayers committed to saving the King's soul and the screams of the damned in the torture chambers of the **Inquisition**.

- Expand Spanish power and influence to safeguard the eternal and immortal—at any cost

- Command the masses, coerce the weak, incite the faithful, torture the heretical— power lies in dominating the people

- Piety, patience, modesty, distrust

William & the Low Countries

Since the expansion of the Roman Empire, the Low Countries have been a nexus of contact and trade. **William I, Prince of Orange**, is sovereign prince within the **Seventeen Provinces**. The cobble-studded lanes of both port and palace alike are filled with opportunity but stained with blood.

Some claim that trade in the region's mercantile houses deals in more than material things—hinting at those who deal in dark thoughts, damned hearts, and virgin souls.

The fresh sea air masks something putrid and half-forgotten. Some who wander these streets seeking their fortunes vanish without a trace as if the cobbles swallowed them up.

- Whatever service you want, whatever item you seek, there will always be someone who can offer it—at a price

- Almost everything can be bought, but trust and loyalty can only be earned

- There be divers sorts of death—some wherein the body remaineth, and in some it vanisheth quite away with the spirit

The Fae of the Great Wood

The great forest—that stretches through the heart of England and across the churning Channel into the heart of Europe—holds memories that precede humanity. The tangle of ancient trees and clawing briars hides a sepulchral heart bound by an oath long forgotten by one side and considered all but spent by the other.

The Great Wood's roots run across the continent, and the **Fae** lay claim to it all, but the oath holds and only fissures leak forth the sap of vengeance. One day, the bough will break, and the Fae, thirsting for their freedom, will take everything back.

- In tradition lie strange truths, hidden paths, untold treasures and myriad portals; to embrace it is not without cost

- Every action has an equal and opposite reaction; humanity has forgotten the quid pro quo that once made the worlds as one

- Offer a simple trade, like-for-like; a heart-for-a-heart, an eye-for-an-eye

Practitioners of the School of Night

The School is a cabal of astronomers, astrologers, artists and scholars, directed by **Sir Walter Raleigh** and the Earl of Northumberland, **Henry Percy**. The existence of the organisation came to light through the loose talk of **Kit Marlowe** and **Will Shakespeare**. Raleigh was the latest in a long line to expand the reach and the influence of this esoteric and ungodly circle.

The School claims origin in Ancient Greece, focusing on devotion to melancholia as a source of artistic and creative nourishment. The truth is more sinister; adherents play host to a tenebrific entity. The entity offers dark insight, spread through ritual induction to new members.

The School's objectives run at odds with many key figures—including Dee—pursuing articles and knowledge of power to nefarious ends.

- Black is the badge of hell, the hue of dungeons and the school of night. Potency lies above, beneath and within the darkness

- Items of esoteric and scientific interest are better held by the School than allowed to "roam free" amidst fools and vulgarians

- Existence is augmented by melancholy and enriched by tragedy

The Tudor Age

The Dee Sanction has the potential to be run with a varied focus. As a gaming group, you need to decide upon the settings' specific values, raising them for authenticity and immersion while never taking your eye off the entertainment and fun. All groups will opt for something different, a mix of feel and flavour that engages everyone at the **Table** in the middle ground.

In Favoured Light

The Tudor period combines pride, arrogance, violence, paranoia, superstition and driving ambition into a dangerous mix. This saw each contender in her Court set firmly against one another to **Queen Elizabeth's** benefit.

At the heart of English power, every member of the Court sought the Queen's ear, and many believed they had it. The Queen knew how to manipulate both people and events. And those who played the game could garner the benefits—though they risked everything in the gamble.

Lord Burghley, **Essex**, **Raleigh** and the others sought favour by impressing the Queen—but all too often, they forgot themselves and overstepped the mark, to their chagrin.

GM and **Players** alike can choose to seek or avoid this searchlight of attention, leaving the business of patronage and good favour to the likes of **Walsingham** and **Dee**. On the other hand, the group may wish to try their hand at diplomacy and build their reputations toward greater things, but they play a high stakes game in doing so.

The **GM** should not hold back from setting high expectations and considerable challenge to attain favour and keep it. **Agents** that fancy the challenge will find their way littered with traps laid by those potential favourites of the Queen. The latter would not readily see their influence diluted.

Not History

Running a game of **The Dee Sanction** shouldn't be comparable with writing a dissertation or sitting a verbal test. No one at the **Table** will be marked for accuracy because we're not dealing with a purist representation of history. Simultaneously, the changes to the environment are not so significant as to generate a completely alternate world.

John Dee used his influence with **Queen Elizabeth** to insert a loophole in magick's legislative presence. He argued the case for the change based on escalating the realm's defences in light of credible intelligence around the esoteric expansion of enemy states.

He furnished himself with the means to pursue his own studies and research into the otherworldly without fear of prosecution. This as much as to spite ne'er-do-wells in the Queen's Court who might take umbrage with him.

Otherwise, history pretty much runs along as-is.

Play your games as a shared storyline using the historical tropes and common understanding from around the **Table**. Without years of education and reading, you can't hope to simulate Tudor England, and you

shouldn't try. The end result, for all the wins in immersion, will likely fail to entertain. Play to the level of authenticity that appeals to and engages everyone.

Conspiracy & Superstition

The period, and Elizabeth's Court, was rife with rumour and promises about the business of alchemy, astrology, witchcraft and similar matters. On the one hand, the statutes made it quite clear that magick would not be tolerated. Yet, many of the nobility, the Queen included, gave patronage to practitioners of occult arts.

Alchemy—and specifically the pursuit of the **Philospher's Stone** as a means to turn base metal to gold and imbue eternal life—plagued the court like a bad case of the Pox. Prophecy had a place in establishing critical dates in the diary—the **Queen** had **Dee** divine the most auspicious date for her own coronation.

However, **The Dee Sanction** assumes that most of the common acts of magick and occultism seen in England's courts and streets amount to nothing more than trickery. Any that pursue plans to raise the dead or summon incubi from beyond have as much chance as anyone. Mostly none at all.

That's not to say that magick isn't real—and that's another lever for the **GM** to manipulate in setting the game's theme and tone. Personally, in writing the game, I envisage a style and tone akin to **The X-Files** or **Fringe**—a world where the strange and uncanny exist, but always at arm's length.

That's the reason why the magick section of this game hints at more than it lists—the threat remains more real the less you prepare for it. Suppose you create specific

and refined mechanics for the occult. In that case, it falls into the realms of either nonsense or science—fakery or something repeatable. **Dee** himself hoped to achieve some measure of this in codifying Enochian—a cypher that could convey the wisdom of angels like maths and geometry so as to solidify our world's scientific certainty in the Universe.

Universal Threat

Monsters are real—fact. Nothing that any mere mortal can do will threaten their existence or undermine their subtle control of the world. With the lever flung and all gauges set to 11, this version of Elizabethan history has more in common with **Hammer Horror** and **Universal** monster movies.

Both magick and the supernatural provide a tantalising mystery, often just out of reach but always a tangible threat. Challenge comes in the form of uncanny manifestations and dire abominations. Herein are werewolves, vampires, angels, demons and the occasional dragon—the sceptics were wrong, the peril is genuine.

GM Tools

Reaction

Where an **Adventure** doesn't note an **NPC's** attitude or where you create an encounter on the fly, roll **1D10** (or **Draw Unblooded**) on the **Reaction** table to provide a random posture toward the **Agents**.

Alternatively, the **GM** can choose one of the options that fit the situation based on **Agent** actions and/or attitude.

D10	REACTION
1	**Flee**: shy, scared, circumspect
2	**Avoid**: guilty, demoralised
3	**Testing**: wary, questioning
4	**Quid Pro Quo**: trade, gossip
5 or 6	**Neutral**: indifferent, undecided
7	**Convert**: subvert, persuade
8	**Mischief**: mislead, ill will
9	**Rob**: deprive, subdue, hinder
10	**Hate**: kill, destroy, sacrifice

Fortune

Players should be under no illusions – the odds are stacked against them. **Agents** often fail, struck by their inherent weakness in the face of forces better prepared or more powerful. Bizarrely, this is all part of the fun!

Each **Player** has a single **Fortune** token to ease their progress. **Players** spend a **Fortune** to re-roll any single throw of the dice, including **Challenges** or a **GM** roll. For example, a **Player** might choose to spend a **Fortune** to force a re-roll of a **Reaction** by an **NPC**.

Each **Player** has their own **Fortune**. Some **Agents** will push too hard, too fast and spend early; others will wait too long and end the **Adventure** with unspent **Fortune**. The option to force a re-roll of any **Die** means you can help a friend—but once gone, it's gone.

This limited supply lasts for a whole **Adventure** (which might be more than a single **Session**). Once they're gone, the **Player** (or **Players**) will have to manage on their own and face the **Consequences** when they **Falter**.

Between **Adventures**, **Fortune** refreshes to the original total.

Complex Consequences

When a character suffers harm, that usually equates, simplistically, to a lost **Hit**.

However, both weapons and hazards have qualities that generate more harrowing and persistent outcomes. In this case, the definition of the source of harm will outline the possibilities and any means of avoidance.

*For example, a taut wire in the woods might cause an **Agent** no harm but force them to acquire the Consequence **Fallen** unless they succeed in a **Physicall Challenge**.*

*On striking, a poisoned dagger will inflict 1 **Hit** and force a **Physicall Challenge** to determine the **Blade Venom**'s effectiveness.*

How the **GM** invokes the additional effect depends on the situation and any barriers for the **Agent** to overcome to allay them. In the meantime, where the **GM** believes the **Consequence** has an impact, they can invoke it to **Step-Down** the **Resource** for a **Challenge** or limit activities until the condition passes.

Consequences might have an obvious out, like standing up if **Fallen**; otherwise, closing a **Scene** will be sufficient to end **one** lingering **Consequence**. Multiple **Consequences** will take longer or necessitate assistance.

Like **Favours** and **Abilities**, **Consequences** have no fixed list of definition or mechanics. When an enemy, hazard or other complication inflicts a **Consequence**, both the **GM** and the **Player** must define reasonable effects and find a practical route to counter or end it.

Use the following as examples for your own:

- **Bleeding**: the wound leaves hands slick and clothes stained. The **Agent** must stem the flow. Blood may impact social interaction, NPC **Reaction**, and grip.

- **Pummelled**: blossoming bruises and aching pain. Movement becomes awkward; concentration difficult. The **Agent** may numb the pain with herbs, or bleeding may relieve the effect.

- **Nauseous**: Sickening trauma; lightheaded and woozy. The **Agent** cannot focus. If exposed to strong smells or visceral content, the **Agent** is liable to vomit. Steady breathing or peppermint may settle the stomach.

Experience

At the end of every other **Adventure**—second, fourth, and so on—an **Agent** acquires a new **Ability** from the eight available at character creation.

Once the **Agent** has six **Abilities**, increase their **Hits** by **one**. The **Player** can then choose an additonal **Occupation**, **Association** and **Focus** from which they can select new **Abilities** as they survive further **Adventures**.

The approach expands the **Agent's** potential without ramping up their potency. They have the tools to better engage with the world and solve encounters without becoming impossible to keep challenged without ever more powerful enemies.

Resolving Hazards

Loosely speaking, **Hazards** are inanimate **Threats**. They lack will or motivation but otherwise function as an enemy. **Hazards** inflict **Hits** and/or **Consequences** under specific conditions, determined by the process of **Resolution** explained below.

The **Hazard table** outlines a few common examples upon which the **GM** can improvise.

Falling—descending from a height will always hurt, but reaction and a forgiving surface might mitigate the outcome. Getting up ends a **Fallen** consequence. A soft landing will reduce the fall by 2 metres.

Disease—a disorder affecting abnormal bodily change. These are short-term and debilitating, rather than terminal. A disease hampers and may modify **Reaction**. The **Symptoms** function like **Consequences**.

Poison—substances that impair health. A **Falter** on the **Challenge** may lead to severe internal damage and, potentially, death.

Burning—exposure to intense heat. If it catches, the **Agent** will **Burn** until they take action to put it out, like immersion in water or rolling around on the ground.

Try to use **Hazards** to remind the Players of their **Agent's** mortality rather than bringing their career to a grinding stop!

The table also includes notes about how **Agents** can seek to mitigate or manage a **Hazard's** effects.

*For example, suppose an **Agent** is on fire. In that case, they will continue to accrue **Burns**—and potentially additional **Hits**—until they take posi-* *tive action to douse the flames, such as jumping into water or rolling around in the dirt.*

Hazard	Resolution
Falling	Any fall of 2 metres or more requires a **Physicall Challenge**. **Falter**: 1 Hit + 1 for every additional 2m fallen; **Else**: 0 Hit + 1 for every additional 2m fallen. In addition, the character lands in a **Fallen** condition, taking a **Moment** to get up.
Disease	Roll D6: **Falter**, nasty; **Else**, benign. Roll **1D8 twice** for **Symptoms**: 1, Fever; 2, Tired; 3, Nauseous; 4, Cough; 5, Congested; 6, Bowel Issue; 7, Aching; 8, Swellings Duration: **3D6** (if Nasty: x2) (**D10**); **Falter**, days; **Else**, hours. Folk name (**choose** or **2d8**): Bloody, Dry, Falling, Great, Green, Jail, Long, Putrid; crust, evil, fever, fires, palsy, pox, sickness, sweats. An **Agent** can look for someone to provide a diagnosis and treatment for a disease. Treatment will cost at least 10 shillings, then **Take A Chance**: cut the duration by 50%, unless the roll **Falters**, in which case the condition sees no improvement.
Poison	**Physicall Challenge**. **Alcohol**: **Falter**, Ko'd 2D4 hrs; **Else**, Step-down all **Resources**; **Lesser Toxin**/Venom: **Falter**, 1 Hit, Seizure; **Else**, Fever & Nausea; **Greater Toxin**/Venom: **Falter**, 1 Hit (**D8**, 1-2 Death, 3-8 +1 Hit), Seizure; **Else**, 1 Hit, **Confused**, **Pained**; an **Agent** with medical expertise can attempt an **Intellectuall Challenge** to provide a treatment or antidote to relieve the negative effects, which will require access to suitable materials, herbs or medication.
Burning	**Sudden, direct heat**: Burned. **Ignition**: (roll D6) **Falter**, catch fire; **Else**, flame dies. **Burn**: 1st Moment, Burned (or 1 Hit, if already 2 x Burned); 2nd +, **Physicall Challenge** or +1 Hit. An **Agent** can put out a fire by forfeiting their action for **two Moments** and either dowsing the flame or rolling around on the ground.

◦○◦

Running the Game

The game isn't meant to be complete; as GM, you should adapt or add to the rules, using the basic principles as your guide. If in doubt, you can **Challenge a Resource** or **Take a Chance**.

Be fair, impartial and always consider it worth engaging the whole **Table** if in doubt. Be sensible; never roll the dice unless it adds drama.

Improvise rather than worry about following the letter of an adventure. If you tie yourself too tightly to written events, you risk dampening the sense of adventure and wonder. Be flexible but consistent.

Troupe Play

Consider using your first session to create a couple of characters for each **Player**, including the **GM**. The speed of character generation makes this a relatively painless and straightforward process.

42

By generating several, a **Player** can replace a deceased **Agent** immediately. Also, they can vary the **Agent** they use to suit the content and focus of the session.

For **Experience** purposes, the **Player** can choose which **Agent** they improve.

Adventure Freely

Don't sweat the preparation because you never know who will make it to the next session. Keep your ideas loose and adapt them to **Player** choices. If you have many basic plots prepped, you can adjust and recycle anything you don't use at a later date.

Use the outcome of adventures as your springboard and ask the **Players** what they plan to do next. As they outnumber you, their decisions should have as much weight, if not more, than yours as **GM**!

Keep Journals

Information you share with the **Players** can be invaluable, so encourage them to keep written records during and between sessions. The deeper the **Players** get into the game's narrative and detail, the more plot potential and richness you, as **GM**, have to build upon.

When you enter a location, meet a familiar face or push into a new thread of the plot, invite the **Players** to fill out the detail. Journals filled with notes of events, people, places and possessions provide both a point of personal reference and a great source for hooks into new adventures and investigations.

One Shots, Chance & Sychronicity

The ebb and flow of **Player** (and indeed **GM**) involvement means that a campaign is often just a connected string of **one shots**—those one-off games that fill a spot in the schedule when **Players** can't make it.

During the game and in-between sessions, consider the personalities and factions that the **Agents** have interacted with and respond to their actions and plans, then develop the ideas for the next session.

Your guiding principle should be, "What are the logical consequences?" But, don't be tied to linear time; consider the events that may have led to adventures that have already happened and how they came about.

Mine the potentials of history, the carefully recorded events in **Player** journals, and the mysteries that arise from random tables and improvisation.

Converting Existing Adventures

The Dee Sanction is a game of investigation, subterfuge, and the supernatural. It can work well with adventures ranging from grim fantasy to modern-day horror investigation.

You can make the process less onerous by extracting the core plotline, events, locations, or whatever else from a pre-written adventure and then build from there. Many games' varying power levels will make a direct conversion a challenge. Recreating enemies and events line-by-line will be more work than the value returned.

Allow an adventure to serve as an aid rather than a straitjacket. Use it as a rough tour rather than a hard-and-fast itinerary. Read books on the period and highlight liberally—on discoveries, personalities and/or events. Each may serve a purpose through your campaign—as backdrop, encounter or diversion. It can be really satisfying when you drop something authentic seamlessly into a game.

Converting Monsters

You have the responsibility to create the challenges and threats that populate the game world. But, you shouldn't worry too much about balance and like-for-like conversions if you run adventures from other game systems.

Focus on creating exciting and unique monsters and opponents, and worry less about whether the **Agents** can handle a fight head on—more fool them if they do.

As a rough guide:

Hits: assume **1 Hit** for every strike a creature could take from a **longsword** with average damage, rounding down.

Potency: a creature with natural dexterity, high natural armour, or other means to overcome attacks will likely have at least ▼1 or ▼2 Potency making physical attacks hard.

Armour: tough armour slows combat down, even where combined with a weak opponent. **Agents** facing a well-protected enemy can consider innovative tactics. **1d12** is weak armour, while **1d4** is tough—like chainmail.

Tradecraft: many systems note a resistance or a vulnerability that can be overcome with the right preparation. Be cautious about making this **Tradecraft** unless the opponent is a significant foe in the adventure. Better to set such a quality as something challenging but manageable instead—like adding an Achilles' Heel—rather than a **Mark**.

Reference

Many books, web sites and essays contributed to the ideas used that brought **The Dee Sanction** to life. The following are just a scattering of recommendations. If you only have time to pick up and study one, choose the first on each sub-list.

John Dee and the Supernatural:

- **The Arch-Conjuror of England, John Dee**, G Parry
- **The Supernatural in Tudor and Stuart England**, D Oldridge
- **John Dee and the Empire of Angels: Enochian Magick and the Occult Roots of the Modern World**, J Louv
- **The Occult Philosophy in the Elizabethan Age**, F Yates
- **Giants, Monsters & Dragons** and **Spirits, Fairies, Leprechauns, & Goblins** by C Rose
- **The Discoverie of Witchcraft**, R Scot

Spies and espionage:

- **The Elizabethan Secret Services**, A Hayne
- **Under the Molehill**, J Bossy

Broadbrush **Tudor history**:

- **The Time Traveller's Guide to Elizabethan England**, I Mortimer
- **The Elizabethan World View**, E M W Tillyard
- **The Tudors in 100 Objects**, J Matusiak
- **Elizabethan's London**, L Picard
- **Elizabethan People**, J Hurstfield and A G R Smith
- **The Princely Courts of Europe 1500–1750**, edited by J Adamson
- **How to be a Tudor: A Dawn-to-Dusk Guide to Everyday Life** by R Goodman

General reading and viewing:

- **The Element Encyclopedia of Secret Societies**, J M Greer
- **A Discovery of Witches**, Sky (Season 2)

Lost in Translation
A One-Shot Adventure for The Dee Sanction

"Come live with me and be my love, And we will all the pleasures prove, That valleys, groves, hills, and fields, Woods, or steepy mountain yields."

— Marlowe: The Passionate Shepherd to his love.

Lost in Translation takes place during the great tour of European courts undertaken by John Dee and Edward Kelley in pursuit of occult knowledge, noble assistance, and the greater understanding of communication with angels. This adventure serves to introduce the common theme that all are shades of grey and that the right answer is often not the easiest. Situating it in the middle of the period serves to introduce the concept of troupe play and keeping journals. However, with minor adjustments the GM can relocate the events to rural England with Dee seeking patronage from an intractable noble or scholar. The eyelash might be his own or one of the other scryers he employed over the years.

Deep Background

Roughly 60 years ago, a devout preacher gave up the calling to marry. He set aside the tools of his faith and took up the plough. A little over a year later, his wife had a son – **Slavomir**.

Ten years later, on the cusp of puberty, that son had a chance encounter while playing in the eaves of the wood on the edge of the farm. The boy chanced upon three **Ladies of the Fae** after he caught himself a nasty gash across the face from a low branch. They soothed his pain and tended to his injury as he held back his tears. The women gained the trust of the lonely child, engaging in kind acts and delighting in games over the coming weeks and months. They offered the boy their hearts, forever, in return for his own and he gave it.

In time, the farm passed from father to son—the parents passed, less than a season apart, and Slavomir was alone. He loved the land and appreciated the hard work. Those long days of childhood faded as the business prospered, but the Ladies would never forget.

When the farmer received the offer of a wife—many years his junior—he took the proposal seriously. Aside from the business of running the farm, he saw the affections of this kind and beautiful woman, **Elena**, as a part of the deal of becoming a man of means, a boost to his standing. He accepted. When she found herself with child, he felt something he hadn't felt in decades, love. A chill fell on a corner of the farm; bright eyes darkened with jealousy.

Not long after the harvest, Slavomir's wife died in her labours. The Fae Ladies spirited away the baby from the womb as Elena lay in her bed and bled to death. The farmer's world fell into ruin; his wife dead and his baby with her. And with them, the land seemed to die too; an unnatural atmosphere settled upon the fields. The farmer lost the will to carry on, but the Ladies wouldn't let him go; he had a promise to keep, forgotten though it might be.

The following spring, the farm receives an unexpected visit — from **the Dee Sanction**.

The Dilemma

Lost in Translation introduces a small situation for the Agents to investigate while in pursuit of a relic. While the adventure kicks off with the characters pursuing the desired item, that object provides a diversion into the situation on **Slavomir's farm**.

A small and unconsidered action set these events in motion; can the Agents recover the forgotten memory and find resolution in the miscommunication between Fae and a lonely child?

The Task at Hand

Doctor Dee, his companion **Edward Kelley**, their wives, and the associated and necessary retinue arrived in **Europe** around the close of **1583**, accompanying Polish nobleman **Albert Laski**. It seemed that Dee might use the trip to open up personal opportunities and strengthen alliances with the nobility of northern and central Europe; alas, Laski proved out of favour, and attempts to have audience with the Emperor and the King of Poland proved fruitless.

April, 1585 — Seeking to convince **King Stefan of Poland** of his good intentions and, what is more, his direct conference with angels, Dee proposes a demonstration. In a secret meeting with the King and Kelley, at the **Stone House** in **Krakow**, he acquires the location of **a forgotten relic** through communion with the angel **Uriel**. As his agents, Dee provides the characters with the challenge of discovery and one of **Kelley's eyelashes** suspended in a sealed bottle of spirits as their "angelic" guide. They must beat a path across the countryside and return with the relic with haste. What could be simpler?

Adventure Path

The Agent's guide brings them to the edge of **Slavomir's farm** after following the road from Krakow through the foulest of Spring weather. The trip takes them south along **a well-travelled road**, frequented by merchants with wary guards, battle-weary soldiers and superstitious peasants — all travelling north to the capital.

Travelling on foot—neither Dee's finances nor King Stefan's goodwill stretch to the provision of horses—takes them more than a day, requiring an overnight stay in an abandoned barn. Just beyond the zenith of the sun— in a sky filled with brooding cloud and relentless rain—the angelic guide swivels west toward a muddy track that leads away into the woods.

From here, the adventure depends on the investigation and interactions of the Agents.

Sensitive Issues

The adventure includes scenes that describe animal negligence, resulting in distress and death, as well as the loss of a child and mother in childbirth. As **GM**, you should be mindful of the possible triggers and discomfort these scenes might present and provide a mechanism to pause or cut scenes—reference John Stavropoulos' X-Card or Brie Sheldon's Script Change Toolbox.

Non-Player Characters

The investigators will interact with a single primary Supporting Character, **Slavomir the Farmer**, for most of the adventure. Aside from the farmer, they may also have encounters with his two helpers, **Mislav** and

Dobrogost, as well as the three nameless **Ladies of the Fae**.

The entire adventure could wind to a conclusion without a single conflict—really, that's the expectation, and a wily group will realise that **The Dee Sanction** isn't about fights. That said, it is often about conflicts of a completely different kind.

The information below outlines these key characters and their characteristics, as well as personal resources should a fight arise.

Slavomir, the Farmer

1 Hit (none), 1 Attack

♥ [1,2] **Weep**: 0 Hits, cry, move away

♣ [3,4] **Plead**: 0 Hits, implore, move away

♦ [5,6] **Flail**: 0 Hits, **Bruised**

♠ [7,8] **Swipe**: 0 Hits, **Bloody Cut**

Slavomir is a **grey-faced**, **broken** man; he has **black-ringed eyes** from sleeplessness, his **spirit visibly broken**. He has a **scar** across his eye, from above the brow to the middle of his cheek.

He treats the Agents as **late guests**—something that might make them wonder whether Dee knew their destination. He didn't, nor can the Agents check this; the Fae presence garbles outward communication. Slavomir has **a note** in his possession—it simply says "**Expect them.**"—and **a pouch with coin**. It was on his doorstep, he says; he can't account for who left it. It's possible that this is a test by Dee; the Agents might, rightly, see this as display of his power.

Slavomir **doesn't answer the door** nor react to the Agents entering the longhouse some other way, like through the windows. He **doesn't speak unless spoken to** and then shares only limited responses.

Pointed questions to the farmer reveal the following information:

• He lives with his **wife**, **Elena**, baby child, and **two helpers**, **Mislav and Dobrogost**.

• **Elena** is **unwell** and **asleep** upstairs. She's been affected with melancholy since the birth of their son.

• His two helpers, **Mislav** and **Dobrogost**, are terrible. They're **lazy** and careless, more concerned about sleep and beer than keeping the farm in order.

• Despite the lack of good help, Slavomir believes that the fortunes of **the farm will turn around** come the next harvest.

If asked about the condition of the fields, his dreadful state, or specifics about his wife and child, he becomes **vague**. He skirts around reference to his child's gender—he genuinely has no idea; he aspired to a son.

For most problems, Slavomir finds it most natural to **place the blame on the farm help**.

Mislav & Dobrogost, the Help

no Hits, no Attacks

Both Mislav and Dobrogost are **dead**, so looking to fight them serves little purpose. **Mislav** was a **foot shorter** and more **heavy set** than Dobrogost. **Dobrogost** had a couple of **secret keepsakes** that the Agents might find if they search the **Barn**.

Evidence of the Farm Helpers remains in two areas:

• Two **scarecrows** surmount the hill behind the longhouse, upon the **Fallow Field**. The scarecrows wear the tattered clothes of the Farm Helpers and one stands a foot taller than the other.

47

- The hay **Barn**, behind the **Longhouse**, hides the **bodies** of the dead men, lying face down on the upper level.

The Help can be useful to break the mood if things get too dark, akin to the comic relief in a Shakespearean play. Even in death, they're hopeful they might yet escape from the Farm.

The **scarecrow curse** also means that their situation can never be permanently changed. Look away and things repair themselves or items return. Piecing together their eternal fate should trigger an **Unravelling** check.

Carrying the Scarecrows down the hill enough times might just piss them off enough to result in a spot of violent animation. Use **Slavomir Hit Resolution** options if you need to determine effects.

The Ladies of the Fae

6 Hits (▼1, 1d8), 3 Attacks

♥ [1,2] **Rapture**: see below

♣ [3,4] **Maddening Voices**: see below

♦ [5,6] **Faithful Fields**: see below

♠ [7,8] **Snowstorm**: see below

Three ethereal Fae. Though referred to as **Ladies**, their appearance and sex is transient; they appear to fit the expectations of beauty that suit the viewer's taste. The default is **Slavomir's**; fragile, pale skinned with a cascade of ill-kept blonde hair — the first and strongest memory of his mother.

If the characters penetrate the Fae Domain (see **Rye Field**, below) and enter the **Longhouse**, they find the **Ladies** there with the baby. In the warmth and light of the farmer's childhood home, the Ladies offer eternal comfort and play for their innocent soulmate. They have nothing to gain from conflict; they have all that they want. **Agents**

cannot hurt them while they remain in the **Longhouse**—the heart of their fragment of the Fae domain.

If the **Agents** lure the **Ladies** out of the **Longhouse**, they will physically retaliate. Inflicting **2 Hits** will put a single **Lady** out of action and **-1 Attacks**. Only if the **Agents** somehow lure the Fae into the real world can they be destroyed utterly.

The Ladies have a **weakness** for making **bargains**; they would pause any violence if the Agents plead their indulgence and enter into meaningful negotiations.

The Ladies have **no concept of time** or references to the passage of it. Yesterday, always, the year, the seasons—it's all meaningless. As **GM**, try to avoid using any terms that relate to the passage of time.

The **relic** has no impact on the Ladies; the Fae domain existed long before this mortal religion. However, like the events earlier in the century, faith is a damper on their influence; removing the relic from the Fae domain will allow their dominion over the location to grow.

- **Faithful Fields** – commanding the land about them to rise up to provide transit, carriage, protection, obstacle, or defence. If used to attack: it inflicts **1 Hit** plus a **Consequence**, as the ground swallows a limb (**Snared**), contorts underfoot (**Sprain**) or churns (**Slowed**). If used to defend, The Ladies **Resistance** improves by one step (**1d6**).

- **Maddening Voices** – casting their voices into the minds of any within their Domain, unless silenced through **Supernaturall** resistance. Brief words can be spoken freely; protracted conversation requires concentration.

- **Rapture** – instilling a sense of absolute joy in a target, leaving them unwilling to engage in violent response while concentration is maintained. The Ladies lose an Attack, while one maintains the effect, but the target cannot act violently toward them. Indeed, the **Rapt** character is more likely to get in the way; roll 1D8 every **Moment** the effect persists, with a **Falter** putting the target in the way.

- **Snowstorm** – whipping up the snowflakes into an elemental storm, dropping the temperature and visibility. Target is **Blinded** and **Chilled**. **Blinded** lasts until after the victim's next action/attack, but **Chilled** persists. If **Chilled** again, take **1 Hit**. If **Chilled** a further time, **Physicall Challenge** or **+1 Hit** (i.e. 2 Hits suffered if a third Chilled effect is suffered and the Challenge fails).

The Farm

Slavomir has worked the land here since his father died. The farm covers some twenty acres of **fields** and **woodland**, supporting a thriving business. The wood provides building material, firewood and a source for foraging and hunting. Last season, Slavomir planted **barley** and **rye**, while keeping the north field fallow.

The place supported him, his wife, two helpers and several dozen animals—**cows**, **goats**, **pigs**, **chickens**. Since the curse settled in the **autumn, 1584**, the help became increasingly alarmed, turning to drink and becoming slack in their labours. The land went untended, the animals' needs forgotten; **Mislav** and **Dobrogost** complained of unnatural encounters, strange noises, and unseasonable weather.

When the **Agents** arrive at the farm, it's a grey late autumnal day, though a moment

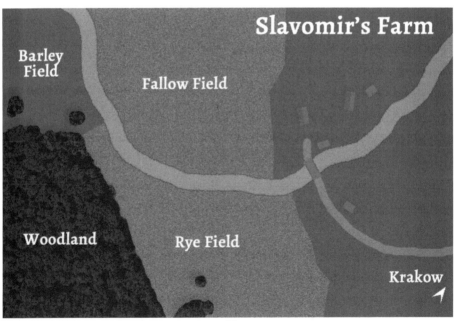

Slavomir's Farm

Barley Field

Fallow Field

Woodland

Rye Field

Krakow

before it will have been a rain-soaked morning in mid-spring. As the farm comes into view, the **Agents** see no sign of life.

Departing the Farm

After 5 minutes on the farm, the Agents will find themselves **unable to leave** (see below). An **unnatural mist** falls around the boundary. Anyone stepping into the fog will find themselves blinded and then emerge at a random spot around the bounds; this triggers an **Unravelling** the first time.

Roll a **1d12**—or draw from a King-free suit—to determine the clockface point at which the **Agent** re-emerges on the edge of the farm (i.e. a 3 means 3 o'clock, on the midpoint of the eastern edge).

If an **Agent** is secured with **rope**, the tether remains intact and can be pulled in either direction. Pulling will tug the pulled to the point where the puller stands.

Common Thematic Traits

While on the farm, the Agents' investigation may uncover details with common traits that tie into the situation and, specifically, the curse on **Slavomir**:

- Standing **water, sluggish and oily**; it feels and acts like jelly rather than liquid

- **Fallen leaves** on the ground suggest autumn, not spring

- **No wild animals**, birds or insects heard or seen within the cursed farm

- **Odour of decay**, hardly perceptible; slow decomposition due to lack of putrefaction or verminous predation

- A **patina of frost** on any bare metal

- A **dry, frigid air** current seems to follow the Agents around

- Indecipherable, **whispered words** that only one person ever seems to hear at any given time (though, see **Barley Field**, below, where words are clear)

Inward Track

- There are **more tracks on the trail inside the farm** than outside the cursed area; the help tried more than once to leave the place, on foot and by cart

- **After 5 minutes**, the Agents **cannot leave** the farm without the **Ladies'** permission or possession of the relic

The main road south of **Krakow** provided easy travel due to good maintenance and fair use. The track the compass guides the **Agents** onto shows far less care; it is rutted and slick. Half a mile off the main road, suddenly the **rain stops** and the **hair in the bottle spins** in a lazy circular motion. The woods that surrounded the Agents thin out, revealing a **sheltered farm** on the side of a **low hill** that rises on the north side.

The hair continues to spin while the characters remain at the farm. Only by accessing the Fae domain does the hair cease to rotate.

The **Agent's Black Amulets**, which typically allow them to reach out to Dee (like a pager), cease to function as communicators. If anyone tries to use an **Amulet**, they sense only silence. If anyone steps back out of the farm, they find that the malfunction continues; the effect of the Fae domain sticks and will not fade until the characters remove the **Amulet** from its influence for 24 hours.

On entering farm, the **Agents** find that a **wall of mist** thickens on the trail behind them. The **rain stops**; on the woodland eaves the ground is **leaf-littered**.

Looking out from inside, the Agents see it **continues raining; looking in**, they can **perceive that difference**. Outside, the road ahead looks rutted and muddy, rain falling. Inside, the land shows **no recent sign of rain**.

After 5 minutes inside the farm, the **Agents cannot leave**. The only way out is with the **Fae Ladies' permission** to leave—something they will offer in return for a reasonable trade—*or* **acquiring the relic**, which suppresses the Fae influence.

Dairy Barn

- **Dilapidated** building, several **splintered timbers** and gaping **holes**

- **Odour of decay**, hardly perceptible

- **Feeble moaning** sound from inside

- **Overturned barrel** of feed

As the characters come along the inward track, a barn stands to their right, short of a **stone bridge** across the river. The Agents can hear a feeble **moaning**. The barn smells of **manure** and **decay**. If the Agents skirt the exterior, they see movement through a hole; a **shrivelled cow's nose** nudges into view.

There an **overturned barrel** with the dregs of feed spilled out near the hole where the cow pokes through. The lower **edge of the hole** is stained dark with **blood**.

The **weathered door** is secured with a loop of rope. In eight stalls the Agents find the skin and bones of seven **dead cattle** and an eighth, emaciated and slumped in a corner, the source of the moaning. The cow's flesh is tight to the bone and blood stained around the front.

The surviving cow, secured in its pen, managed to smash a gap in the timber to reach the feed barrel, lacerating its flesh as it strained out through the hole. The animal will greedily feed if released.

The **smell is unpleasant**, but strange. The animals died from malnutrition; the **carcasses rotted abnormally**.

Agents with **medical** or **veterinary expertise** can see that the animals show **no sign of disease** or abuse, they **starved** to death. The **carcasses'** state is **unnatural**. After a month, the body would normally have flattened and liquified. After two, only a skeleton would remain.

The Stone Bridge

- Sturdy **stone arch**; very **old**

- Square marking in the soil, on the right before the trail meets the bridge; like a **large post mark**

- Sluggish, **oily water**; no fish or birds

The bridge pre-dates the farm. The river flows east to west, but at the moment flow would be an inappropriate term. The water passes under the bridge like **oily jelly**; it gurgles, but does not froth or ripple. Scooping water from the river leaves a hole of sorts; drinking the **water is safe**, but odd.

The **post mark** is about a foot square. Digging beneath the soil, there is the **remains of a timber box**—which clearly extended into a sort of cabinet above ground. The base is weighted with rocks; pieces of splintered wood might be found if the earth around the post is dug through.

This was a **shrine**, which Slavomir's father constructed when he gave up the life of a preacher. It once held the **relic**—a bone-coloured **splinter of wood**. Both shrine and the relic are long gone; the **eyelash spins** lazily here, as everywhere else on the farm.

Animal Pens

- Open pens; sturdy wooden fences. Part of the **fence** has been **battered** to the ground

- Pens are **filthy**; buckets for **feed empty**

- Flesh stripped **chicken carcasses**

A selection of **pigs**, **chickens** and **goats** were penned here, close to the river near the bridge. All of the animals look **underfed**, but are **roaming free**. One of the pigs battered the fence down and upended a feed barrel.

Feed buckets in the pens contain murky, oil-streaked rainwater. The animals have stripped the ground clean down to the dirt. The pigs ate some of the chickens, accounting for the carcasses and scattered bones.

A **curious chicken** keeps an eye on the Agents every movement near the **Bridge**.

Barn

- **Substantial building** of seasoned timber with a **slanted roof**

- Big **double door**, **facing the river**, secured with a leather loop

- A **trail** runs between here and the front of the longhouse; rutted with tracks

- **Odour of decay**, hardly perceptible

The **ruts of a cart** show, as well as **footprints** from at least three people of differing size and build.

Inside, there are a couple of **barrels** that give off a smell of small beer, both empty. **Straw** litters much of the ground, some stacked in **bales** around the edges. A **horseshoe upper floor** offers more storage space accessed by a **ladder** on the south wall.

There's a **pitchfork** by the barrels. The **cart** is set to one side, under the eaves of the upper floor, covered by a **tarpaulin**.

A search of the ground level in the north of the barn finds **rough pallet beds** with coarse blankets. The beds **stink of sweat** and **urine**; one has a **leather purse** beneath the **bedding**, containing two **copper coins** and **a small bone cross**. The eyelash doesn't react to the crucifix; this is not the relic.

Ground level on the west side, there's a **patch of darkened straw** beneath **stained timbers** above. Both straw and ground have soaked up considerable amounts of **blood**.

Investigating above, via the ladder, uncovers the bodies of the **farm help**, side-by-side. They have **blood stained clothes**, their throats cut with awkward shallow strokes. Two **blood-dark knives** lie in the straw.

Whether the PCs encounter the **Scarecrows** before or after finding the bodies, they recognise the identical clothes. The **Fae Ladies** cursed **Mislav** and **Dobrogost** for their attempt to escape through suicide, binding their souls to the turnip-headed **guardians of the Fallow Field**.

Store

- **Stone** and **timber** construction

A short distance from the **Barn** is a storehouse. The door isn't secured. Inside the Agents can find essential farm tools and standard supplies, like **lanterns**, **oil**, **rope**, and so forth. The store contains nothing of significant value. In a pinch, characters can use most of the tools as makeshift weapons.

If you need a fright or confrontation for the Agents, the Store can be home to **a swarm of ravens**. On opening the Store, the birds fly out in an angry swirling cloud, directly into the faces of the unsuspecting. If the Agents have entered the Store already, the inexplicable appearance of the birds will prove even more confounding.

An **Agent** releasing the **ravens** should immediately piece together—if they haven't already—the complete lack of wildlife on the Farm. Once released and aloft, they vanish completely.

Longhouse

- **Substantial hall** of pale **wood** and **thatch**; signs of age and **poor upkeep**

- **Main trail ends** here; a further trail, mainly of footprints and lighter cart wheel tracks, heads north along the river side

- **Small square windows**, **shuttered** and **curtained**, on the ground level. Larger windows, on the upper level

- Only **one entrance**, **secured** from within; no answer to calls or knocks

- **Odour of decay**, hardly perceptible

The **longhouse** dominates the centre of the farm, sitting in an area of well-trodden ground at the **end of the track**. **Knocks** go **unanswered**. The **door** is **secured** with a bar from the inside; Slavomir got tired of the farm help coming in to complain.

There are **narrow windows** on both levels, each with outer **shutters** and **curtains**. An Agent can **squeeze through**, though they would be vulnerable as they did so.

The building has an open **hall-like** interior, with a **long table** in the middle with a half dozen chairs. A **horseshoe platform above** can be accessed by a **narrow stair** on the western side. A **stone-cold fire pit** sits behind the table. There are **straw beds** on both sides of the fire pit; a good supply of **firewood** sits unused. Two **doorways at the back** lead into a kitchen and a pantry.

The stair leads up to a **walkway** that circles the building, with a store of basic materials and supplies—including **blankets** and a couple of **lanterns**—at the front and the farmer's **bedroom** at the back.

The **table** is set for a **meal**, but the cooked meat is cold, the **milk turning**, and the **bread going hard**. The room **smells** of sweat and something ripe—**sweet** and **unsettling**. **Slavomir** sits at the head of the table and mutters, not raising his eyes from the table as they enter—*"You're late."*

Slavomir insist the Agents are late, explaining he had **a letter** delivered, on the door step, a couple of days ago, with a payment in coin. He will show them, both the message—"**Expect them.**"—and the **pouch**. He offers a place to sleep—on the cots—and that they can help themselves to food. He asks them not to raise their voices, not wishing to disturb **Elena**, who is resting.

Slavomir looks both tired and hungry, but will accept neither sleep nor food. There's no *objective*—public—time passing, only *subjective*—personal. He has moments of disorientation, but feels compelled to wait until night before he rests. The curse, however, means all humankind on the farm need neither sleep nor food to live.

If the Agents need assistance with something outside the longhouse, Slavomir suggests they ask the **farm help**, though he can't account for their location. *"They're lazy and feckless, what more can I say."*

The Kitchen

- **Messy**, with the scattered remains and utensils of breakfast

- All **food** here is **dry** and **shrivelled**, or on the turn toward going off

There's nothing rotten here that would account for the smell in the main room. Stale and dried vegetables and bread might be fit for the animals, but nothing more.

The Bedroom

- Drawn curtains veil the room in **shadow**; movement raises **dust**

- **Sparse furnishing**, with everything set in place; in line or in parallel

- **Odour of decay**, hardly perceptible; slow decomposition

- A **bed**, clearly occupied, a **travel chest**, and a **cot**, incomplete and empty

Slavomir insists that the Agents not disturb his **wife**, but a distraction or simply moving faster than him—easy considering his weakened, sleepless state—will allow someone to investigate. The other option would be to climb in through one of the windows on the upper level, requiring a **Physicall Challenge** to avoid a 2 metres fall.

The interior lies in shadow, the curtains pulled. The air reeks of decay. On entering, anyone can see that someone occupies the bed, but they don't move and there's a dark stain clearly visible on the sheets.

Elena is dead. The bedding, her shift, and her skin are all bloodstained. It's clear that she's been dead for some time, but decomposition makes it hard to judge.

Anyone with an appropriate occupation can ascertain that she **died in childbirth**; a discomforting and unpleasant examination can determine that there is **no sign of a baby**.

The **travel chest** contains **spare clothes**—both male and female—as well as a hand woven blanket intended for the cot.

There is a **dresser** close to the window on the east side. As well as a **mirror**, there's a **prayer book**, in Latin, and a **silver crucifix**—neither is the relic the Agents seek.

Barley Field

- **Untended field** grizzly with stubble, the severed stalks mottled and dark

- Chill and **unnatural breeze**

The field furthest from the **Longhouse** comprises acres of rough ground peppered with dark and diseased stalks. Post-harvest the field would normally be cleared and prepared for new planting, but not here. A chill wind whistles through the scabrous stems.

The Agent with the highest **Supernaturall Resource** standing in these areas or upon the east bank of the river bordering the area can catch a whispered warning carried on the wind: "**He is ours.**" If Agents share the same high value, they all hear it.

Woodland

- **Unnatural mist** billows between trunks

Agents standing within the eaves of the woods find them **devoid of wildlife**. Focussed in silence, they catch **faint birdsong** or the **muffled cry** of foxes, heard from a distance.

Whether or not you used the encounter at the Store, you may have **a swarm of ravens** emerge suddenly and violently from the haze. **Supernaturall Challenge** to perceive that the action and shape of the swarm precisely mirrors that already seen, almost like a repeated vision.

Anyone entering the woods proper experiences dislocation, as described under **Departing the Farm**.

Fallow Field

- **Gentle rise** toward the northern bounds

- Soft, **uneven ground** with sprouts of wild grass

- Two **figures observe** from the north edge

The field stands idle, a **gentle hill** rising to woods that rim the northern edge of the farm. Surveying the field from the southern area of the farm, the Agents spy **two observers** on the far north edge. One, the taller of the two, waves. The distance—it's almost 200 metres to the top of the field—and the mist at the edge of the wood makes it **difficult to pick out details** until the Agents close the gap by at least two-thirds.

Agents walking up the field will find the ground soft and uneven, making progress difficult. The figures wait in silence, unresponsive to calls or gestures. When the Agents get close enough, they can see these are two **scarecrows**, one slightly shorter than the other. Both have large **turnip heads** and wear **tatty cast-offs**.

If the characters have been into the **barn**, they will recognise the clothes as belonging to the **farm help**, **Mislav** and **Dobrogost**.

A search of the scarecrows finds a **purse** containing **two copper coins**. The purse and coins are identical to those found in the **Barn**. This may trigger a realisation about the Farm Help—and the curse upon them—triggering an **Unravelling**.

Once the Agents move away, the scarecrows animate—two figures standing together, one of them waving. If someone stays close, they continue to see the scarecrows but get the **creeping sense of being watched**.

Carrying the **scarecrows** down the hill will work; but the moment the Agents take their attention off them, they disappear and return to their position.

The Agents could burn or chop up the scarecrows, but the moment they're left unattended the remains disappear and the figures return on top of the field.

Coins in the purse do not endlessly regenerate—they too disappear when attention slides.

If the Agents survey the whole farm from the top of the **Fallow Field**, they can see an odd **pale patch** in the **Rye Field** near the mist-cloaked woods across the river. The Agents can't make out what it is without direct investigation.

Rye Field

- **Untended field** grizzly with stubble, the severed stalks mottled and dark

- Chill and **unnatural breeze**

On the south side of the farm—on the same side of the river as the track leading in—a field of **ragged stalks** is all that remains of the rye field. A **fringe of tree** surround the southern and western edge. A chill breeze carries across the field from the dark of the **Woodland**.

If the characters **search the field**—or survey it from the **Fallow Field**—they see a **pale patch** on the west side. A flurry of **snow** hangs above the patch, like a haze of dust in a stream of sunlight. The patch is **two yards square**, such that from the edge no one can reach into the middle without stepping in. Simply reaching into the patch dusts limbs or objects with snow, which melts slowly.

An Agent who steps inside immediately enters the **Fae Domain**; anyone outside the patch can no longer see them. Reaching into the area of the patch isn't enough for the transition to take place; a character must step inside before they then vanish.

The Fae Ladies' Domain

- **Snowing** from a **cloudless** sky, filled with **stars**; a **bright full moon**

- **Winter** landscape, heavy with snow, identical to the farm

- Light from the **Longhouse** blazes like a **beacon** in the dark

The landscape of the **Fae** resembles a picture postcard winter view of **Slavomir**'s childhood. This domain snapshots the instant that the farmer pledged his heart to the **Fae Ladies** and that moment lives forever.

It's snowing, a bright moon shining in a clear sky filled with stars. The PCs can see the familiar buildings beyond the river, light spilling out of all the Longhouse's windows.

They stand in a well-tended field, maintained and ready for new growth. The patch of ground where the Agents appear is the only area not snow-covered, though the flakes start to settle. Thick, powdery snow covers everything. In the distance, near the bridge, a child attempts to build a snowman.

The **boy** will not startle. **Dressed warmly**, cheeks rosy, he seems unaware of the cold. A livid **scar** runs from above his left eye to mid-cheek, recent but healing.

South of the bridge—near the point where Slavomir labours over his snowman—a narrow **wooden post**, like a free-standing alcove, is an obvious change to the other farm. Someone has painted the back of the alcove with a crude image of the **Virgin Mary** holding the baby **Christ**. The shelf of the alcove holds several small offerings—coins, flowers, morsels of food—surrounding a shallow brass plate. A **sliver of pale wood**, almost bone coloured, sits on the plate. If an Agent possesses supernatural sensitivity, or holds out the **compass**, it becomes clear that this is the **relic** they have been seeking.

The boy doesn't recognise the Agents. If asked about the relic, he explains that it belongs to **his father** who placed it there when he set up as a farmer. If asked about his parents, he says they've gone to market. He doesn't seem certain about it nor does he know when they will return. He isn't lying, he just doesn't know.

If asked about his home, he's happy to invite the strangers in, to warm themselves by the fire. The **Longhouse** is identical to the one the characters have seen, but in much better condition. The boy will let himself in and leave the door open for them to follow.

Inside, the central table and all the other furnishings look the same. At the head of the table, nearest the kitchen, three **Fae Ladies**—possessed of ethereal beauty and of indeterminate age—sit together. The central Lady cradles a **baby**, in swaddling clothes; the babe coos as the Fae sing a song.

The **Fae** act with arrogance and indifference. As the Agents may have heard them whisper on the wind, "He is ours."—they means both the farmer and his son. **Young Slavomir** anchors them here; he is their eternal beloved. They have claimed the baby for their own, by right of this eternal link.

They're open to discussion, but any debate about Slavomir—young or old—or the baby has little weight. The **Fae** have all the bargaining chips, so what can the Agents offer them?

Possible interactions with the **Fae Ladies**:

- **Sacrifice**—one of the Agent can offer themselves in exchange for Slavomir *or* the baby. In principle, the Players might realise that such an exchange will break the original agreement. They won't see the truth of it until they leave the Fae Domain, but the exchange will be permanent. Rescuing the **Young Slavomir** will return the baby to their arms as they emerge into the real world, but the **Fae Domain** will persist and their companion will remain lost to the **Ladies**.

  Sacrifice need not be as extreme as leaving an Agent. The Fae Ladies will consider other **bargains**. An Agent might **give up** the ability to love, lose their smile, or hand over their memories of a special person.

- **Fealty** - the **Ladies** will invite the characters to **partake of a meal** with them. Anyone with **Fae knowledge** or who makes an **Intellectuall Challenge** will be aware that taking anything will create a **Fae bond**. If they accept and consume any of the food or drink, they will be bound to owe the **Ladies** their honour and a significant favour. In return, they will consider giving up something—the same principle as above applies, i.e. just the boy *or* the baby.

- **Conflict** - a fight is less of an offer and more of an ultimatum. The Agents can battle the **Ladies** to return the young boy and the baby.

The **GM** should handle the conflict with narrative care using the details of the **Ladies** provided at the start of the adventure. The **Ladies** have nothing to gain from conflict, so they're more likely to fight defensively and attempt to force the **Agents** out of their realm. Their supernatural abilities support this approach, using the environment to force the **Agents** away.

The **Relic** means nothing to the **Ladies**. They have no recognition or understanding of human faith; they predate humanity's existence, and religion means nothing to them. If the **Agents** ask to take the **Relic**, the **Ladies** will answer, "*The what?*"; **Agents** can take it without argument or resistance.

Take note that the **Relic** has served a purpose here; its presence contained the **Fae Domains'** spread, else the **Fae Lady's** influence might have spread.

If the characters take the **Relic** with them, they remove the one thing that has curtailed **Fae Lady's** power over the area for more than half a century.

To return to the real world through the spot in the field is possible, but the **Agents** must first wait for the snow to cover the patch. It takes **15 minutes** of **game time** to coat evenly with new snow, and then they can return as they arrived.

Stepping back, the **Agents** will discover the outcome of their decisions and the elements recovered from the **Fae Domain**.

In Conclusion

This adventure intentionally leaves the endgame open. The potential for a moral quandary is ever-present.

If the **Agents** rescue the baby, they achieve something, but the **Fae Domain's** influence remains, and **Slavomir** cannot leave the **Farm**.

If they leave the baby with him, he will care for it, but the characters have achieved little. In time, the **Fae Ladies** will find a way to reclaim both man and child.

If they rescue the boy, they break the **Fae Ladies'** hold over the man; **Slavomir** can go. The **Agents** may need to drag him away for his own good, but he can't put up much of a fight. However, he has lost his grip on reality; only forcing him to confront it, such as showing him his dead wife, might suffice to bring him back.

If the **Agents** retrieve the **Relic**, they succeed in the mission; it will allow **Dee** to gain a foothold in the court at Krakow but at a significant cost. With the **Relic** gone, the dominion of the **Fae** expands over the coming months, creeping out across the wilderness toward civilisation.

In time, the **Emperor's seat** will be threatened by the advancing influence of the **Fae Domain**. One day, the **Dee Sanction** will need to return and set things right...

If the **Agents** leave the Farm by the **Inward Track** *without returning*, they venture into the **Great Wood**. They will become lost—if this is a one-shot—else, their return from the **Fae** realm will require a quest to uncover some means of return to the real world.

Possessions

Agents can scrounge fair quality tools to support the Abilities of their prior occupation. Other than that, choose THREE tables, and roll 1d10 on each.

As well as a knife, you carry your trusty...

Weapon

1	Cudgel
2	Short Staff
3	Wooden Stake
4	Swiss Dagger
5	Sickle
6	Shortsword
7	Small-headed Mace
8	Short-chained Flail
9	Horse Whip
10	Well-notched Cutlass

Though not essential, you have a...

Tool

1	Ball of Twine
2	Bone Toothpick
3	Padlock and Key
4	Tallow Candle wrapped in canvas
5	Chain
6	Jar of foul-smelling grease
7	Large Scissors
8	Metal Spike
9	Shovel
10	Short pole

Fruit of the local printing press, you have a...

Printed Matter

1	Concise local travel pamphlet
2	Complicated recipe
3	Page torn from an Almanac
4	Love ballad by a little known poet
5	Verse for a gloomy part-song
6	Loose leaf from an edifying treatise
7	Provocative hagiographic critique
8	8th imprint of a Lutheran testimony
9	Cryptic genealogy
10	Reproduction of a letter

You prize a family heirloom that's...

Keepsakes

1	Old
2	Miniature
3	Fragile
4	Damaged
5	Heretical
6	Disguised
7	Visibly repaired
8	Impractically embellished
9	Clearly made by a child
10	Garish

As well as your day-to-day clothes, you have a...

Clothing

1	Leather Belt with hoops
2	Wool socks
3	Ring
4	Travel cloak
5	Wool coat
6	Fancy Hat
7	Locket
8	Silk scarf
9	Good boots
10	Bracelet

Probably has a story attached, you carry a...

Odds and Ends

1	Numbered key
2	Bone comb
3	Glass eye
4	Loaded dice
5	Carved wooden figurine
6	Human tooth
7	Sealed letter
8	Game piece
9	Foreign coin
10	Small wooden spoon

Manors & Mannerisms

Roll d12 (or A♣ through 12/Q♣), then d6 (or 1/2 ♥, 3/4 ♠, 5/6 ♦)

Home Town

1♣	♥London | ♠Norwich| ♦Cambridge	7♣	♥Worcester | ♠Lincoln| ♦Hereford
2♣	♥Newcastle | ♠Coventry| ♦Exeter	8♣	♥Gloucester | ♠Leicester| ♦Hadleigh
3♣	♥Salisbury | ♠Ipswich| ♦King's Lynn	9♣	♥Great Yarmouth | ♠Dover| ♦Oxford
4♣	♥Canterbury | ♠Totnes| ♦Reading	10♣	♥Southampton | ♠Bolton| ♦Bristol
5♣	♥Colchester | ♠Lavenham| ♦Wisbech	11♣	♥Wrexham | ♠Carmarthen| ♦Brecon
6♣	♥Bury St. Edmunds | ♠Hull| ♦York	12♣	♥Dublin | ♠Drogheda| ♦Waterford

Roll d4, then d12 (or draw a card from a King/Joker-free deck)

Phlegm ♦

1	Easy going attitude
2	Quietly stubborn
3	Doesn't want to be any trouble
4	Avoid conflict
5	Open to all the options
6	Passive listener (I am listening!)
7	Can't we all just get along?
8	Unevenly apportions work
9	Watches others
10	Avoids making decisions
11	Always looking for the exits
12	Easily amused

Black Bile ♣

1	Reserved
2	Generally looks sad or upset
3	It's safer not to go alone
4	Schedule orientated
5	Hears negatives
6	Avoids criticism
7	Incredibly organised
8	Difficult to please
9	Suspicious
10	Always with a flourish
11	It's always better to music
12	Thrifty

Yellow Bile ♦

1	Eager to find out more
2	Unreasonably ambitious
3	Insistent (go on, go on...)
4	Trustworthy
5	Louder is better
6	Always prepared
7	Knows everything
8	Unrepentent
9	Self-sufficient (but not prepared)
10	Not tired (but tired)
11	Throws things, just to cope
12	Unnecessarily competitive

Blood ♥

1	Disorganised
2	Short attention span
3	Wealthy in my friends
4	Sudden emotional pendulum
5	Credit where credit's due
6	Wants to please
7	Unintentionally forgetful
8	Open to being led astray
9	Generally full of cheer
10	Have gossip, will gossip
11	Mildly immature
12	Always tries to bounce back

Random Names

A message sent to @MrGarland4 provides an alternative approach to quickly generate a character.

2D12	Male (♦ ♥ / ♣ ♠)	Female (♦ ♥ / ♣ ♠)	Surname (♦ / ♥ / ♣ / ♠)
2	John / Leonard	Elizabeth / Christina	Abell / Chatwyn / Grimbald / Morecote
3	Thomas / Martin	Joan / Edith	Abery / Cheddar / Haddock / Mugge
4	William / Simon	Margaret / Emma	Adams / Chester / Harte / Nash
5	Robert / Peter	Agnes / Lucy	Alington / Child / Harwood / Oke
6	Richard / Philip	Alice / Marion	Ashton / Clark / Hatteclyff / Page
7	Henry / Stephen	Anne / Cecily	Askew / Cole / Hodgeson / Petley
8	George / Lawrence	Mary / Grace	Aubrey / Conquest / Hornebolt / Pyn
9	Edward / Roger	Jane / Amy	Aylmer / Daunce / Hylderley / Roper
10	James / Daniel	Catherine / Rachel	Bacon / Dickinson / Irving / Sandes
11	Francis / Michael	Elinor / Charity	Bailey / Duff / Killigrew / Scrogs
12	Nicholas / Samuel	Isabel / Rose	Ballard / Egerton / Knoyll / Shawe
13	Ralph / Allen	Dorothy / Fortune	Bands / Estney / Lake / Shevington
14	Christopher / Charles	Margery / Judith	Barfoot / Fitzlewis / Leeds / Snell
15	Anthony / Alexander	Susanna / Philippa	Barton / Fletcher / Lloyd / Sparrow
16	Matthew / Gregory	Ellen / Audrey	Berry / Fox / Lodyngton / Stokerton
17	Edmund / Nathaniel	Sarah / Janet	Bewley / Froste / Lond / Sumner
18	Walter / David	Frances / Sybil	Boothe / Gage / Loveryk / Treningham
19	Hugh / Luke	Joyce / Beatrice	Borrow / Geffray / Lyon / Ufford
20	Andrew / Tobias	Ruth / Maria	Bray / Godfrey / Lytton / Vawdrey
21	Humphrey / Isaac	Constance / Blanche	Carter / Goldwell / Mede / Warde
22	Abraham / Ambrose	Amphelisia / Lettice	Cavell / Gomfrey / Merstun / Winter
23	Barnaby / Griffin	Kynborow / Faith	Cely / Goodryke / Milner / Wyard
24	Valentine / Squally	Clarice / Charity	Chase / Gorste / Molyngton / Yaxley

Bestiary

Black Dog – 5 Hits (▼1, M)

Huge, black hound that haunts remote trails and churchyards in search of the lost and the unwary. Pony-tall, wild, and with eyes the size of saucers.

♥ [1,2] **Hell's Gust**: 0 Hits, **Bruised**

♣ [3,4] **Maul**: 1 Hit, **Sprain**

♦ [5,6] **Sulferous Bite**: 1 Hit, **Burned**

♠ [7,8] **Bestial Snap**: 2 Hits

Doombinding: anyone looking a **Black Dog** in the eyes must **Take a Chance** at the end of combat. To fight blind, ▼+2. If they **Falter**, the **GM** rolls and records the result of **1D6+1**. In that many days time, the unlucky soul suffers harm equal to the result of the **Take a Chance** in **Hits** (i.e. 1 to 3).

Phantom: the **Black Dog** can expend two **Moments** to pass through a barrier, whether wood, stone or common metal. It cannot breach a magic ward (**M**) nor become a phantom within one; a blessing provides no such protection. It can choose to remain a Phantom, but cannot cause physical harm in that state. Silent movement; leaves no tracks or trail.

Attacks: can make **two attacks** per **Moment**.

Fire Drake – 8 Hits (▼3, MV)

Fiery meteor, animated and baleful; a cavalcade of blazing air that flits with dire exuberance.

♥ [1,2] **Fiery Haze**: 1 Hit; **Phy Ch.**, if **Falter**: then **Burned**

♣ [3,4] **Blaze**: 1 Hit; **Take a Chance** for all nearby, **Falter**: **Dazzled**, lose next **Action**, ▼1 for the following **Action**.

♦ [5,6] **Flaming Lance**: 3 Hits

♠ [7,8] **Outburst**: erupts, sears all creatures within 10 yards; 1 Hit, **Phy Ch.**, if **Falter**: 3 Hits.

Meteor's Path: Flyer. Capable of moving at great speed; it can move to or from a distant point by expending a whole **Moment**, to (or from) the range of a long bow/matchlock (about 200 yds).

Insensate: immune to burning, cold, poison, disease, charm, and similar mortal weaknesses.

Splash Down: suffers **1 Hit** in harm for every Moment immersed in water. Dissipates temporarily at 0 Hits. If lured (**V**) and weakened (**M**), immersion extinguishes the Drake permanently.

Guttering Flame: if weakened (**M**), **Drake** stat line becomes ~ 6 Hits (▼2, **MV**).

Ghoul – 4 Hits (▼1, 1d12)

Grave encrusted wanderers, dressed in the crypt-stained finery of nobility. All too common a sight along the streets and lanes of the Low Countries.

♥ [1,2] **Épée Flick**: 0 Hits; feint gives ▼+1 **Resist** vs. opponent until end of next **Moment**

♣ [3,4] **Tomb Fetor**: 0 Hits; **Phy Ch.**, **Falter**: lose next Action vomiting

♦ [5,6] **Vile Barb**: 1 Hit, **Lesser Toxin**

♠ [7,8] **Greedy Hook**: 1 Hit; sinks teeth and claws into noisome grapple; **Agent** can either fight on at ▼ 1 Phy Ch. or tear free for **+1 Hit**

Raised Properly: gifted with dark sight; receptive to rational exchange.

Insensate: immune to cold, poison, disease, charm, drowning and similar mortal weaknesses.

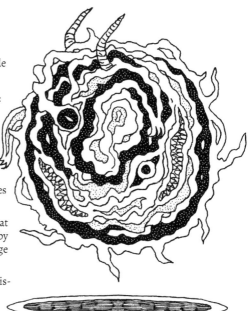

Will o' the Smith – 4 Hits (†, **A**)

Condemned soul—crooked and elderly—that lights the way for travellers with a hellfire lantern, seeking to end them down hazardous routes.

♥ [1,2] **False Path**: 0 Hits; **Sup Ch.**, **Falter**: for next **Moment**, walk away from your focus/fight

♣ [3,4] **Soft Ground**: 0 Hits; thick mud saps the target's strength, **Fatigued**

♦ [5,6] **Tormenting Fire**: 1 Hit. Coruscating hellfire envelopes the target; **Sup Ch.**, **Falter**: **Panic**, lose next Action

♠ [7,8] **Devils Breath**: 1 Hit; anyone within 5 yards of the **Smith** is must **Take a Chance**; **Falter**: **Burned**

Coal Lamp: a piece of the **Smith's** hellbound soul fuels its lamp, a gift from the Devil. An **Agent** can render the **Smith** powerless by immersing the coal in water thrice-blessed by a Catholic priest (**A**). While in possession of the lamp, **Will o' the Smith** can **Take a Chance** when anyone takes harm nearby, **Success**: regain 1 **Hit**. The hellish artefact dissolves to a sulphurous lump when the **Smith** dies.

Spirit (†): immune to common physical contact and unable to interact physically itself; vulnerable to magical or blessed objects that might cause harm.

Insensate: immune to burning, cold, poison, disease, charm, fatigue, drowning and similar mortal weaknesses.

Goblin – 4 Hits (1d8, **A**)

Misshapen imp risen from the spilled blood of a fallen Fae; mischievous and hungry.

♥ [1,2] **Blood**: 0 Hits, **Spattered**

♣ [3,4] **Corpse Dirt**: 0 Hits, **Nausea**; **Phy Ch.**, if **Falter**: then ▼ 1 **Phy Ch.** next **Moment**

♦ [5,6] **Mire**: 0 Hits, **Bleeding**

♠ [7,8] **Blood Puppet**: 0 Hits, **Bleeding**; **Sup Ch.**, **Falter**: suffer -1 **Phy** until rest. If **Phy** is zero, the **Goblin** instead can dictate the target's **Action** in the next **Moment** (see below).

Blood Leap: can travel between blood pools, which usually litter the environment it inhabits. Else, it can travel up to 200 yards. Movement takes less than a Moment and the Goblin awareness, with all senses, extends to both pools while in transit. The Goblin can attack through the surface of a pool, requiring the target **Sup Ch.** else suffer a free strike.

Regenerate: while in contact with blood, the **Goblin** recovers 1 **Hit**, to 4 max., at the end of a **Moment**.

Spatter, Not Swipe: immune to mundane edge weapons.

Blood Puppet: manifests as a blood trail between Goblin and puppet. Target must check **Sup Ch.** at ▼ 1 or act according to the Goblin's whim. Even if successful, the Action is lost, but the influence is broken. An Agent can also intercede to end the puppetry by knocking the target out or severing the link with a fae-forged silver blade.

Severe the Ties: like common fetches, to summon a **Goblin** is to bind with blood. A fae-forged silver blade (**A**) – or, at a pinch, a cutting tool improvised from fae silver, can severe the regenerative link the **Goblin** has to its master and render it vulnerable to complete dissolution.

Hag – 4 Hits (1d10)

A human twisted by the taint of the Fae in the Great Wood; a wicked and twisted magick wielder.

♥ [1,2] **Mock**: 0 Hits; **Sup Ch.** for all who can hear the witch, **Falter**: **Panic**, lose next Action

♣ [3,4] **Heartless**: 1 Hit; target seizes and gasps, heart pounding. Next **Phy Ch.**, roll twice and take worst result.

◆ [5,6] **Evil Eye**: 1 Hit; target ▼1 on **all Challenges** until after their next **Action**

♠ [7,8] **Hex**: 1 Hit; plus 1 Hit to another target within 10 yards.

Glamour: cloaked in magick, the Hag can appear in any human guise. The change is perceptional rather than physical, so contact with the creature may break the spell. Check **Sup Ch.** at ▼1 to see through the disguise—those with some means of supernatural perception check without step down.

Far Sight: the **Hag** can see, with concentration, through the eyes of vermin, anything within ½ mile.

Mare – 5 Hits (1d8)

Grotesque cherubic gnome that launches itself upon a sleeping target and presses the life from them. Light as a feather or heavy as a horse.

♥ [1,2] **Fade**: 0 Hits, **Make Distance**

♣ [3,4] **Fatigue**: 0 Hits; **Phy Ch.**, **Falter**: fall **Asleep**; can be awakened with a sudden shock.

◆ [5,6] **Pulverize**: 1 Hit

♠ [7,8] **Flying Rush**: a prodigious leap, at a target up to 10 yards away; check ▼1 **Phy Ch.**, if **Falter**: 2 Hits and **Fallen**; else, 1 Hit.

Dream Stuff: a **Mare** can dissipate by expending a **Moment's** effort. While invisible, it remains physically present, but cannot interact without becoming visible again. It can **Pulverize** as a surprise attack, forcing ▼1 **Phy Ch.** to defend.

Feather to Boulder: a **Mare** can adjust its weight instantly, to maximise damage, survive a fall, or avoid being picked up and removed from a victim.

Oaken – 5 Hits (1d8)

Headless, barrel-chested fae brutes that seek revenge in the material realm for the destruction of trees from the Great Wood.

♥ [1,2] **Root Grasp**: 0 Hits; **Phy Ch.**, if **Falter**: then **Entangled**

♣ [3,4] **Thrash**: 1 Hit

◆ [5,6] **Rake**: 1 Hit, **Bleeding**

♠ [7,8] **Thorn Grip**: 1 Hit; entangle opponent with brambled branchlets; Agent can either fight on at ▼1 **Phy Ch.** or tear free for +1 Hit

Oaken Form: while motionless, they blend in seamlessly with other plants; even in motion they're difficult to spot from a distance, ▼1. They cannot be harmed by non-magical weapons in this state.

Headless: Oaken sense their surroundings using their roots, aware of everything in contact with the ground within 5 yards. Attacks that blind or deafen are ineffective.

Rooted: Oaken spread and withdraw a network of root filaments with every step. The stability means they cannot be knocked prone or made to stumble when stationary, only if in motion; ▼1 **Phy Ch.** to strike them while moving and unmoored.

Zmaj Vuk – 7 Hits (▼2, 1d8, CKV)

Ravenous flame-eyed shapeshifting progeny of the despot Vuk Grgurevic. Hulking wolfling gifted with aristocratic and draconic blood.

♥ [1,2] **Lacerate**: 1 Hit, Bleeding

♣ [3,4] **Putrid Bite**: 2 Hits, **Bloody Fever**

◆ [5,6] **Raging Tear**: 3 Hits

♠ [7,8] **Grisly Surge**: 3 Hits, recover 1 **Hit**

Disgorge: an everted wolfskin, with shrivelled viscera intact, confers the **Vuk** with its power. Regurgitating the innards restores their mortal—and vulnerable—human form.

Uncovering (**C**) the identity and location of the **Vuk** in human form and finding (**V**) the skin, the Agents can then treat it with powdered moon-infused hazel husk (**K**) to destroy it.

Bloody Fever: a **Vuk's** bite infects victims with aches and delirium. Infected dead return as **Graveshorn** minions bound to the creature's will [2 Hits, (1d10), **Insensate** as *Ghoul*].

Grisly Surge: raining eviscerating blows down upon their enemies, the **Vuk** draw sustenance from the gush of vital fluids—recovering **1 Hit**, as noted.

Dual Swipe: when they strike for **3 Hits**, the **Vuk** can split the wound 2/1 upon their current opponent and another nearby target.

Attacks: Vuk have **two attacks** per **Moment**.

Assassin – 3 Hits (1d12) *shadowy assailant*
Soldier – 3 Hits (▼1, 1d8) *mercenary-for-hire*
Upright Man – 4 Hits (1d12) *master beggar*

While a commoner might be just 2 Hits (none), assuming they justified a stat line at all, Agents will invariably find themselves pitted against those more capable, prepared or supported.

From shadowy **Assassins** tasked with felling the Agents one by one to the **Upright Man**, crafty leader of the homeless keen to better their lot, notable personalities have greater expertise and more options at their disposal.

♥ [1,2] **Back Off**: 0 Hits, **Make Distance**

♣ [3,4] **Graze**: 0 Hits, **Bleeding**

♦ [5,6] **Solid Strike**: 1 Hit

♠ [7,8] **Telling Blow**: 1 Hit, **Special**

Assassin—Side-swiped (Special): slicing unexpectedly or feinting followed up with a stab; Agent can either fight at ▼1 Phy Ch. on their next Action or sustain a 1-2: Deep wound, **+1 Hit**; 3-4: **Lesser Toxin**; 5-6: **Bleeding**.

Soldier—Fortunes of War: as a seasoned fighter, tempered in the chaos of war, the **Soldier** can force the **re-roll** of any single die over the course of a fight, as if spending a **Fortune** token.

Upright Man—Ill-Favoured: in possession of a hex—retained in memory—identical in effect to a **Favour**. Choose or randomise; hex can be reused once per **Scene**.

Upright Man—Followers: an Upright Man commands 4d6 **Vagrants**—2 Hits (none). They will follow orders, but never put their lives at obvious risk.

Boneless – 7 Hits (▼1, 1d8)

Amorphous stream of gore and gristle; overwhelms the unwary to ingest their skeletons.

♥ [1,2] **Stink**: 0 Hits, **Nausea**; **Phy Ch.**, if **Falter**: then ▼1 **Phy Ch.** next **Moment**

♣ [3,4] **Splashdown**: 1 Hit; douses target from above then splashes outward toward all creatures within 5 yard diameter; **Phy Ch.**, if **Falter**: 1 Hit, including original target.

♦ [5,6] **Clinging**: 1 Hit; **Phy Ch.**, if **Falter**: grapples target and swings them as a weapon at other victim within 3 yards. Second target must make ▼1 **Phy Ch.** (as if attacked), if **Falter**: both original target and victim, 1 Hit; original released and **Fallen**, whatever the outcome.

♠ [7,8] **Engulf**: 2 Hits; **Phy Ch.**, if **Falter**: then target becomes trapped and the **Boneless** starts the process of dissolution, **-1 Hit** until zero and then **-1 Phy Ch.** Thereafter. **Engulfed** victim can only try to escape (**Phy Ch.**) until free or the creature dies

Insensate: immune to burning, cold, poison, disease, charm, fatigue, drowning and similar mortal weaknesses.

Glossary of Terms

Ability—learned skills or expertise.

Advantage or **Disadvantage**—sum of factors that modify the difficulty of a **Challenge**.

Agents—the Player Characters (PCs).

Back Story—an Agent's history; their **Occupation**, **Association**, **Focus** and **Favours**.

Call to Fail—if a **Step Down** leaves a **Challenge** below **D4**, a Player can choose to step away or achieve some small thing but always get hurt. The **GM** must outline the price of failure.

Challenge—an activity that involves chance to find the measure of success. Abbreviation: **Ch.**

Character—a Player (**PC**) or a Non-Player (**NPC**) character. The Game Moderator (**GM**) runs all of the **NPCs**.

Consequence—a result less serious than a **Hit**; penalises **Challenges** until rested or removed.

Draw—use **Cards** instead of **Dice**. For a **Challenge Draw** count out cards equal to the Die size, then replace two with **Jokers**. To **Draw Unblooded** use a single Suit without Royalty (Jack/Queen/King). **Double**, **Triple** or **Full Unblooded** mean using additional Suits.

Deplete—use up **Tradecraft** to cancel a **Mark**.

Enemy—an animate **Threat**, like a soldier.

Falter—a result of **1 or 2** (or **Jokers**), **Fails Forward**. This means success at a price—such as a complication or a **Consequence**.

Fortune—a token spent to re-roll any **Die**.

Goal—a compound action ("do *x* and *y*") taken in a single **Moment** of combat.

Hazard—an inanimate **Threat**, like a trap.

Hit—a single unit of harm.

Mark—one or more **Tradecraft** associated with overcoming an **Enemy**, **Hazard** or event.

Moment—a period of 10 seconds.

Resistance—the means by which antagonists avoids harm; *potency, armour* and *Tradecraft*.

Resource—one of three core **Agent** qualities, **Phy**sicall, **Int**ellectual and **Su**pernaturall.

Session—a single meeting to play. The conclusion of an **Adventure** might take more than one **Session**.

Step—adjusting the size of the **Die** for a task, either **Step-Up** (▲) or **Step-Down** (▼). A Step may be more than one, e.g. ▼2. ▼+# indicates an increased effect, so ▼1 and ▼+1 = ▼2.

Table—everyone playing the game.

Take a Chance—a "coin" throw to determine a result.

Threat—anything a **GM** uses to hurt or hinder the **Agents**, including **Enemies** or **Hazards**.

Tradecraft—Access, Conspiracy, Kit, Magick, System and Vigilance; shortened to **ACKMSV**.

Unravelling—it represents an **Agent's** loss of equilibrium as their humours become unbalanced. Narratively, the Unravelling is the weakening walls of reality.

Justice of the Peace—administered justice for minor crimes, poor relief & road maintenance.

Lord Lieutenant—county official; controlled local militia, supervised the **Justices**, and reported events up to the **Privy Council**.

Overseer of the Poor—reporting to **Justices**; responsible for the collection of taxes and the dispersion of charity to the unemployed.

Parish Constable and the Watch—responsible to the **Justices**. Handled the business of street patrols and dealing with criminals.

Privy Council—body of advisors appointed by the **Queen**; included Secretary of State, Lord Treasurer, Lord High Admiral, Keeper of the Great Seal, and the Lord Chamberlian.

Sheriff—lesser local official charged with handling legal affairs, such as handling prisoners.

Patrons of Dee

Favoured of the Queen

Mark Buckley, Carl Clare, Simon Taylor, Nigel Clarke, Newt Newport, David Paterson, Jason Behnke, Chris Miles, Jörgen Bengtsson, Martin Glassborow, Dirk the Dice, Daniel Gregory, Pookie UK, Nathan Merritt, Andrew "Doc" Cowie, Joerg Sterner, Mike Shepherd, Patrick Wilhelmi, Matthew Tyler-Jones, therecusant, Katherine Young, James Turner, Peter Tracy, Benn Mace, Bruce Laing, Stuart Chaplin, Joshua Rush, Donald W., Rick Howard, Zak Ralston

Agents of Dee

Andrew Jones (Backer #1), Pete Bounous, Julian Hayley, Ian Griffiths, Eugene 'Tinman' Doherty, Paul Baldwin, Paul Mitchener, Phillip Bailey, Dom Mooney, Lee Carnell, Robert Mills, Jean-Christophe Cubertafon, Andrew Gronosky, Phil Dicemechanic, Stephen Whitehead, Marc Mileur Le Plaine, Fred Kiesche, Mark Caldwell, Annemarie B., Bonhomie Games, Steve Dempsey, Andy Sangar, Pete Griffith, Matthew Broome, Guy Milner, Philip Glass, Brian Robson, Peter Regan, Claude Féry, Andrew Weir - TheDiceShopOnline, M. Trout, Vintage RPG, Simon English, Brian Suskind, Sebastien Hauguel, Adam Rosser, Ian Hawthorne, Ed Kiernan, Jay Law, Justin "Magnus Vanskelig" Mitchell, Dawid "Dievas" Wojcieszynski, Gary Pennington, Jonathan Powell, Tuomas Ristimäki, Nathan Fuhr, Martin Cookson, S.R. Davey, Kit Kindred, James Cruise, Sam Vail, w. David Lewis, Bud's RPG review, Paul Tomes, Martin Pickett, Michael Cule, Graham Harper, Zac Bir, Schubacca, J&L Candalino, Franklin Shea, Scott Joest/Orcusdorkus, Lisa Padol, Richard Squire, Ian Woodley, Alex Genn-Bash, David Paul, Adam Alexander, Jon Cohorn, Rick Neal, John Wilson, Sam Zeitlin, Isaac VanDuyn, Jim "jwmuk" McCarthy, Chris Berger, Patrick Riley, Ian geronimo Brumby, Andrew Eynon, Peter Larsen, Brian Isikoff, Mel H., Rodolphe Duhil, Jason Tampake, Rodney Basler, Matthew Cole, Christopher P. Crossley, Debbie Bagg, Steve Hill, James R. Wallace, Charles Wilkins, Jon Hodgson, Morgengabe, Steven Ward, Michael Owen Hill, Robert T. Cunniff, Thomas Powell, Jeremy Hiers, Marlies Moore

Mister Garland's Runners

Alexander "N8flug" Siegelin, Andrew Smith, Mark Threlfall, Fin Patterson, Steven Fujisaka, Roland Cooke, Brett Slocum, Nick Carruthers, Rafal Posnik, Dr Andy Lewis, Brian Cooksey, Chris Green, Andy Way, RPGs & Baby Makes 3, David Woods, Johnathan L Bingham, Shawn Stroud, Björn Butzen, Marty Chodorek, Tristan Ravn Salazar, Craig Hindle, Paul Anderson, Patrick Carrick, James Leigh Done, David Morris, Ian McFarlin, Essaire, Rhyer, Jason RB Morton

Traders of the Ossulstone Hundred

Rafe Trevelyan, Stepkin Proudman, the Draper, Rupert Dalton, Ned Fuller, Androwe Hilliard, Edward Kiernan, Thomas Earl Holdsteady, Hermes Lyall, I. B. TOMES & SONS, William Blowharder, Tomas Brace, Mrs Harriet Jacques, Jacob Greenaway, "Mocking" Jay Weiss, Andrew Jones, John Briskyn, Godwin Waterhouse, Walter Sowlbeech, Thomas Swift